P9-BZB-490

What Parents and Grandparents Are Saying About Baby Signs . . .

This book changed our lives.

I cannot emphasize enough how valuable this book is. It was so wonderful to be able to communicate clearly and specifically with our daughter in the months before her now incredible verbal abilities blossomed forth. Baby Signs *truly provides a window into your baby's mind. I urge all parents of young babies to put these signs to work for you.*

—A reader from Northern California

A must-read for every parent who cares!

We have used this book with both of our sons. Our oldest (now three) has a larger vocabulary than most five-year-olds. Even our pediatrician commented on his vocabulary skills. But all of this is secondary to just being able to meet the needs of our kids. We know if they are hungry, tired, thirsty, or need a diaper change.

—A reader from Cincinnati, Ohio

The most rewarding experience of parenting!

Communicating with your baby or toddler before he or she can speak is so amazing! My first child learned over fifty signs by age fifteen months. This is a very easy book to read; it has excellent sign suggestions and illustrations in the back of the book.

—A reader from Chicago, Illinois

This is a very important childcare book!

I'm a language development specialist and an English teacher, and I love to see the way this method encourages the formation of language concepts in my baby's mind. She's been "saying" three-word sentences since thirteen months, and the level of bonding and reduction of what-does-that-baby-need stress has been remarkable.

—A reader from Central California

Best investment for you and your child!

There is no end to my amazement at how much this little guy of mine is capable of. This book is an incredible tool for any parent interested in opening the lines of communication with her baby.

—A reader from Holland, Michigan

A great concept, simply presented!

This book was one of the greatest things to happen to me as a parent. Using Baby Signs *is amazing. I gained so much respect for my son and had such a great time using* Baby Signs *with him. He could express his needs, his desires, his ideas, and even make a few jokes and puns. Now my son is two and a half, and he constantly amazes people because he can speak and think like a four- or five-year-old. I credit* Baby Signs.

—A reader from Dallas, Texas

I can talk to my baby before my baby can talk!

I originally had this book with my now five-year-old. By the time he talked, he was using over forty practical signs. He was talking in sentences by age two. I have a fourteen-month-old son who also uses many signs—and makes up his own! It is so wonderful to be able to communicate with my baby. He tells me what he sees, hears, wants, and how he feels—at fourteen months old!

—A reader from California

Delivers what it promises!

I started using the signs with my daughter when she was eight months. When she was ten months, she suddenly started signing. They were right about babies talking sooner and better with signing. My daughter would combine signs and words by the time she was one year old and talked in sentences by the time she was two.

—A reader from Poplar Bluff, Missouri

Must-have for parents!

I cannot say enough about this book and all that it has added to our relationship with our little ones. Both of my children, now two and four, are very verbal and have been able to express themselves from very early on. This book is well worth the investment—being able to meet their needs and communicate with our children is priceless!

—A reader from Naperville, Illinois

It works, it works, it works!

I bought this when my baby was just a couple of months old. We started signing a few things at six months. My son can tell me when he wants a drink, and when he wants a snack, etc. I love this! Try it. It takes consistency, but it is worth it!

—A reader from Eastern Iowa

The best thing I've done for my child!

I think signing with my baby is the single most important thing I have done to enhance her development and our relationship. Baby Signs has enriched our lives in so many amazing ways!

—A reader from Dallas, Texas

Forgo the frustration!

Baby Signs *is a wonderful book! My daughter began doing the signs at eight months and by thirteen months knew about forty! We did not have the frustration in communicating the way our friends seemed to. I had so much fun with my daughter that I also used it for my son with great success. A really fun resource!*

—A reader from Wisconsin

Required reading for every parent and grandparent!

This book should be given to every parent before they can leave the hospital. The deceptively simple approach to nonverbal communication with children in the nine- to twenty-four-month range presented here is nothing short of magic! My grandchildren can tell us when they are hungry or thirsty, the water is too hot or cold, and if they want more.

—A reader from Chicago, Illinois

BABY SIGNS

How to Talk with Your Baby
Before Your Baby Can Talk

LINDA ACREDOLO, PH.D., AND SUSAN GOODWYN, PH.D.

New York Chicago San Francisco Lisbon London Madrid Mexico City
Milan New Delhi San Juan Seoul Singapore Sydney Toronto

The McGraw·Hill Companies

Library of Congress Cataloging-in-Publication Data

Acredolo, Linda P.
    Baby signs : how to talk with your baby before your baby can talk / Linda
Acredolo, and Susan Goodwyn with Doug Abrams. — 3rd ed.
      p.   cm.
    Includes bibliographical references.
    ISBN-13: 978-0-07-161503-7 (alk. paper)
    ISBN-10: 0-07-161503-2 (alk. paper)
    1. Nonverbal communication in children.   2. Nonverbal communication
in infants.   3. Interpersonal communication in children.   4. Interpersonal
communication in infants.   5. Infants—Language.   6. Child rearing.
    I. Goodwyn, Susan.   II. Abrams, Douglas.   III. Title.

    BF723.C57A27   2009
    419'.1—dc22   2008042536

Copyright © 2009 by Linda Acredolo and Susan Goodwyn. All rights reserved. Printed
in the United States of America. Except as permitted under the United States Copyright
Act of 1976, no part of this publication may be reproduced or distributed in any form
or by any means, or stored in a database or retrieval system, without the prior written
permission of the publisher.

1 2 3 4 5 6 7 8 9 10 11 12 13 14 15 16 17 18 19 20 21 DOC/DOC 0 9

ISBN 978-0-07-161503-7
MHID   0-07-161503-2

Graphic design: Christine Dobrei (www.dobreidesigns.com)
Project manager: Linda Easton-Waller
Glossary photography: Justin Probus

McGraw-Hill books are available at special quantity discounts to use as premiums and
sales promotions, or for use in corporate training programs. For more information,
please write to the Director of Special Sales, Professional Publishing, McGraw-Hill, Two
Penn Plaza, New York, NY 10121-2298. Or contact your local bookstore.

This book is printed on acid-free paper.

Contents

Foreword

AS A PEDIATRICIAN, I FREQUENTLY HEAR FROM PARENTS WHOSE sweet, easy-going nine-month-old has suddenly turned into a demanding and easily frustrated twelve- to eighteen-month-old. We used to blame this transformation vaguely on the "terrible twos" (despite the fact that it's the highly unusual child who waits until age two). Much of the tantruming we see in the second year results directly or indirectly from children not being able to communicate. Just as is true for all of us, not being able to let people know what they need, feel, or think about leaves children extremely frustrated. Unlike us, however, they are left with few alternatives but to scream louder and cry harder.

Now parents don't need to simply endure this difficult time. Thanks to *Baby Signs*, and the two decades of carefully conducted research upon which it is based, parents finally have a wonderful tool to help their children who want so badly to communicate but whose vocal skills have not developed enough to do so. Like an increasing number of pediatricians around the country, I strongly encourage parents to use the Baby Signs program. Just as we have learned that nursing is important for nurturing your baby's body, we now know that signing is important for nurturing your baby's mind and heart.

As a clinician and a researcher, I have been particularly impressed with the systematic way the authors have studied the effects of signing on children's development. Their scientific research, funded by the National Institutes of Health, has demonstrated that by using signs, babies can communicate their needs and desires months before most babies otherwise can do so verbally.

In addition, the Baby Signs program helps babies learn to talk sooner. It also boosts their self-esteem and allows them to develop their emotional awareness. Beyond the developmental benefits to the baby, parents report how much fun they have with their baby and how thrilling it is to explore the world together using signs.

Whether you want to help your child express her needs before she can talk, help her convey her emotions, or help her boost her intellectual development, the Baby Signs program is one of the best things you can do for your baby. That's why I recommend *Baby Signs* to new parents and why I enthusiastically recommend it to you.

—Robin Hansen, M.D., FAAP

Dr. Hansen is a pediatrician and chief of Developmental-Behavioral Pediatrics at the University of California School of Medicine. She is also co-chair of the Education Committee for the Society of Developmental Behavioral Pediatrics and a member of the American Academy of Pediatrics Section of Developmental Behavioral Pediatrics.

Preface

OVER THE PAST TWO DECADES WE HAVE INTRODUCED HUNDREDS of thousands of parents, teachers, and pediatricians to the advantages of the Baby Signs program. Invariably, the response has been amazement at the simplicity of the program and enthusiasm about the many benefits signing can bring to babies and their families. Even our most vocal skeptics have been won over after seeing a baby signing—purposefully communicating to his mom that he wants a cracker, needs more juice, is feeling too hot, or sees a bird up in the tree. It is amazing what little hands and minds can do if given the tools (signs) they need to "tell" us what they know. But where did our own enthusiasm come from? Who convinced us that signs were indeed something special?

How the Baby Signs Program Began

It started on a summer day in 1982 when Linda and her twelve-month-old daughter, Kate, were out in the garden. Enchanted by the colorful blooms all around her, Kate pointed to a rose bush, wrinkled up her nose, and sniffed repeatedly. Life with children often slows parents down long enough to "smell the roses," and Linda had often picked them for Kate to smell, all the while saying things like "See the flower, Kate! See the pretty flower!" Clearly, Kate remembered the connection between the sniffing action and the object, and she trusted that the adults around her would, too. For the rest of the day Kate continued wrinkling her nose and sniffing, which was her sign for all kinds of flowers—in the house, on her clothes, and in pictures in her books. Kate continued to borrow or create signs for other things she wanted to talk about, such as fish, elephants, monkeys, swings, slides, and balls. It wasn't until two weeks later that we realized the significance of what Kate was doing.

Out of Our Living Room, into Our Laboratory

As child development researchers, we were eager to see whether other infants were using signs, too. To find the answer, we began systematically interviewing parents to find out whether their babies spontaneously created signs, as Kate had done. Within days of starting our interviews, the answer was clear. Not only did many parents give us examples of signs their babies were using, but the babies themselves would occasionally interrupt our visit to "talk" to Mom, including a sign or two in the process.

We learned a great deal from these families. And the more we learned, the more convinced we became that babies are eager to communicate and that their creation of signs is a natural part of day-to-day family life. Many babies seemed to spontaneously develop at least a few signs beyond the universal *bye-bye*, *yes*, and *no*, usually between nine and twenty-four months of age. We also noticed that some babies took to the idea with enthusiasm, creating an impressive variety of signs for favorite objects and important needs. Invariably, these babies had families who shared their enthusiasm and encouraged the signing. Moreover, it tended to be the case that the more signs an infant used, the faster that child learned to talk. This was our best clue yet about the effect of the Baby Signs program on spoken language development. Signing seemed, if anything, to speed up the process.

It was at this point that we knew we needed to figure out a way to help babies along. Thus, we began encouraging parents to purposefully teach their babies a few more signs to help them communicate their basic needs, feelings, and interests—anything their babies wanted or needed to "talk" about—until they could talk well enough to communicate with words. And the Baby Signs program was born!

The Original Baby Signs Program

The Baby Signs program began with baby-created signs—simple movements and gestures that babies themselves took from their routine experiences with the people and things around them. Drawing from songs, games, or playful interactions with toys and other objects, babies were finding ways to "talk" before they could talk. For example, several babies we observed twisted their index fingertips together to label spiders—real spiders, pictures of spiders, and even plastic toy spiders. What these babies had in common, we discovered, was the experience of learning the song "Eensy-Weensy Spider" (also known as "Itsy-Bitsy Spider"), along with the hand gestures that accompany key words, like *spider*, *rain*, and *sun*. Other babies, we found, stuck their tongues out and "panted" to call their parents' attention to dogs—clearly an imitation of what they saw real dogs doing. Creations such as these not only provided indisputable evidence of how smart babies are, they also showed just how strongly motivated babies are to communicate with the people around them.

In these early years, before signing with hearing babies was a well-accepted practice, some parents were reluctant to try signing because, as they told us, their babies were not deaf. At that time, signing was seen as a means of communication only for people with hearing impairments. On the other hand, parents were eager to try using signs that our research had shown came *naturally* for babies. So we provided parents with fifty "sign suggestions," simple signs that we had seen babies in our research studies create. We also encouraged parents to watch for their own baby's creations and to create signs themselves when the need arose. This first approach to helping parents get started with our Baby Signs program became the heart of the first edition of this *Baby Signs* book. Published in 1996, it launched the extraordinary Baby Signs movement, which has revolutionized the way today's parents communicate with their babies before their babies can talk.

The Baby Signs Program Evolves

As signing with hearing babies became more popular, parents became eager to teach their babies more signs. As a way to expand their own signing repertoires, some parents turned to American Sign Language (ASL), the official language of the Deaf community, with its extensive vocabulary of established signs. We were thrilled to see parents so excited about enhancing their signing experiences, and we continue to strongly support parents who want to teach their babies the signs of ASL.

To embrace parents' enthusiastic response to signing, we revised the Baby Signs program to increase the number of sign suggestions from fifty to one hundred—about 80 percent of which were ASL signs, with the other 20 percent being either slightly modified ASL signs or alternative "baby-friendly" signs. The second edition of the book was published in 2002 to introduce this newly expanded program to parents throughout the world.

Signing with Hearing Babies: A Worldwide Movement

Little did we know in 1982 that the Baby Signs program would become a worldwide movement. Baby Signs workshops, classes, and trainings are now offered in over forty countries, and Baby Signs books and products have been translated into almost twenty foreign languages. Throughout this amazing growth, our mission has remained the same—to bring the benefits of the Baby Signs program to as many families as possible.

To achieve our mission, we formed the Baby Signs Institute to continue our research on the ways in which the Baby Signs program influences children's development and to design curricula for signing workshops and classes. We now offer the Baby Signs Parent Workshop to introduce parents to the benefits of signing with their babies; two six-week sessions of Sign, Say & Play classes to give parents and babies fun and interactive ways to learn signs together; and an early childhood educator training to help child development centers incorporate the Baby Signs program into their infant and toddler classrooms.

We also founded Baby Signs, Inc., to create developmentally appropriate books, toys, music CDs, and videos for children and educational signing resources for parents and caregivers. A listing of these products, along with detailed descriptions and purchasing information, is included in Appendix D of this book.

We are especially proud of our Baby Signs DVDs. In moderate amounts and with developmentally appropriate content, videos can be a positive source of learning for young children. Our strategy in developing these videos was to keep the time short and the content high quality and educational—including animated and real signing children from whom babies can learn to sign themselves. We have also made sure that the audio and visual elements of these DVDs are fun, engaging, and, most of all, in tune with babies' developing abilities. We have accomplished this through the use of animation, delightful puppets, happy babies, and careful attention to pacing and repetition.

The Baby Signs Program: Right for Every Family

Some families, we have found, want to teach their babies ASL signs only. Other families prefer a more flexible approach and choose to include a few modified ASL signs to make them easier for their babies' little hands to master. And still other families really value the freedom to create signs that work best for their own babies—signs that their babies can easily do to communicate about things important in their own family's daily interactions. Because we love helping all families find the best way to start signing with their babies, we continually revise the Baby Signs program in order to meet these families' various needs.

Our major goal for this new edition is to introduce our new Baby Signs program, which offers an all-ASL approach for the many families who want to introduce their child to this rich and vital language. At the same time, it also includes a set of baby-friendly alternative signs and strategies for families who prefer a more flexible approach. In other words, the Baby Signs program now meets the needs of all families who want to quickly and easily begin experiencing the joys that signing with their baby can bring.

This new edition has also provided us the opportunity to update the Baby Signs research sections, including exciting findings regarding signing and emotional development and the impact of the Baby Signs program in childcare centers and childhood enrichment programs. In fact, we have included a new appendix that describes what we know about using the Baby Signs program in child development centers, the benefits specific to the children and teachers in childcare programs, and advice for helping your child's center become a certified Baby Signs Center.

And, best of all, this new edition comes with a free offer for a copy of our newest *Baby Signs Video Dictionary* DVD, a $19.99 retail value. This instructional DVD includes demonstrations of 150 ASL signs and 35 baby-friendly signs, each easily accessible through just a touch of your remote control. Details for getting your free copy are included in the back of the book, so be sure to take advantage of this super teaching aid.

It gives us great pleasure to bring this new edition to you, to share what we have learned through many years of study about communicating with babies, and to envision the look of sheer delight on your face when you see your baby make her first sign. Teaching your baby to sign is truly a gift—a gift from you to her that will serve her well for years to come.

Happy Signing,

Linda and Susan

CHAPTER 1

Introducing the Baby Signs Program

Carlotta was sound asleep when her inner "mommy alarm" went off. Fifteen-month-old Sophia was crying. Hurrying into her daughter's room, Carlotta noticed immediately that Sophia was desperately and repeatedly blowing air through her lips, her sign for hot. *"Are you hot, sweetie?" asked Carlotta, surprised because the room was actually quite chilly. When the blowing and crying continued unabated, Carlotta felt Sophia's forehead and discovered the source of her daughter's distress: "Oh, you've got a fever!" Some medicine, water, and lots of cuddles later, Sophia was content to settle back down in her crib.*

HAVING A SICK CHILD IS AN UPSETTING AND WORRISOME experience for all parents. Because very young children can't talk, parents often have to resort to guessing what's wrong. Is he teething? Does she have an earache? Is he cold or wet or simply lonely? In this story, Sophia, long before she could say the word *hot*, was able to tell her mother exactly what she was feeling.

The signs Sophia and hundreds of thousands of other babies around the world are using are based on both extensive child development research and old-fashioned common sense about how babies communicate. All babies learn to wave a hand for *bye-bye*, shake the head back and forth for *no*, and nod the head up and down for *yes*. These conventional gestures are just three examples of the many simple, easy-to-remember signs that babies can learn and use to talk about things in their world that they don't have words for yet. Unfortunately, most parents never appreciate their baby's ability to learn additional signs beyond *bye-bye*, *yes*, and *no* that could help them communicate in ways that otherwise would be impossible until they can speak.

Talking is so easy for adults that we forget how difficult it was to learn. When a baby finally produces a true word, he is demonstrating an impressive degree of mastery over all the large and small body parts necessary to make the particular sounds involved. There's the tongue to place, the lips to form, the vocal chords to control, the breathing to regulate, and much more. The reason for "baby talk"—those difficult-to-decipher words, such as "wawa" for *water*—is that babies are physically unable to string together necessary sounds in the word but are doing their best to practice. It takes time, often until they are three years old, before they have mastered their vocal chords enough to make them do exactly what they want them to do.

Considering how slowly babies learn even easy words like *ball* and *doggie*, let alone difficult words like *scared* or *elephant*, many months are lost that could have been spent having rich and rewarding interactions, both for the child and the parent. Thirteen-month-old Jennifer's experience of "reading along" with her father is a wonderful example of the joy that comes from successful communication.

Jennifer loves books. As her dad, Mark, settles on the couch after dinner, she toddles over. Holding her palms together facing up, she opens and closes them, making the sign for book. *Mark's immediate, "Oh, OK. Go get a book to read," satisfies her, and she soon returns with her favorite book of animal pictures, cuddles up close, and begins turning the pages. With delight, she looks at a picture, scrapes her fingers across her chest, and looks up with a broad smile at Mark. "Yep, you're right! That's a zebra!" Mark says. The next page brings Jennifer's finger to her nose with an up-down motion and a proud "Yep, that's an elephant!" from Mark. As the pages turn, Jennifer bounces her torso up and down, opens her mouth wide, tilting her head back, and rubs her hands together. Without hesitation Mark acknowledges that in each case she is right again: "That is a kangaroo," "That is a hippopotamus," and "That is water the hippo is swimming in." They continue through the book, pride clearly showing in both their eyes.*

It doesn't matter how big or little you are—successful communication with other people makes life better. In fact, for the young, who are dependent on their parents for everything, it can even be the link to their survival and well-being.

Is the Baby Signs Program Good for Babies?

Imagine how frustrating it would be if you were unable to talk and had no way to express your needs, fears, and thoughts about the world. You would feel as if you were locked in solitary confinement. Babies can feel this same way, which is why they so frequently throw tantrums and use whatever means they have—especially pointing and crying—to try to convey what they are thinking and wanting. Daily life with a preverbal baby tests everyone's patience, but more than two decades of research have consistently shown us that the Baby Signs program can make bringing up baby an easier and more fun experience.

What's more, our research has proven that signing is actually good for babies. In a large-scale study funded by the National Institutes of Health, we observed 103 families with eleven-month-old babies for two years. One-third of these families were encouraged to use signs; the other two-thirds were not. Our plan was to compare the groups periodically using standardized verbal language and cognitive tests to see whether the Baby Signs experience was having any significant effects—good, bad, or indifferent.

So what did we find? In a nutshell, the signing babies outperformed the other babies in comparison after comparison. They scored higher in intelligence tests, understood more words, had larger vocabularies, and engaged in more sophisticated play. (For more details about the research, see Appendix B.)

Benefits for You and Your Baby

Most gratifying of all, however, were the ways parents described the experience of using the Baby Signs program. They talked enthusiastically about advantages we were expecting: increased communication, decreased frustration, and an enriched parent-infant bond. However, they also alerted us to many more subtle advantages we hadn't considered, like increased self-confidence and interest in books. Here are some of the benefits of signing revealed in our research, benefits you and your baby can expect to enjoy, too.

Benefit 1: Decreases Tears and Makes Family Life Easier

Signing alleviates frustration and avoids the need for a baby to depend on pointing, crying, or an urgent "Uh! Uh! Uh!" to get a message across. The story of Sophia demonstrated how using signs helped a preverbal baby tell her mother what she was experiencing and what she needed. Parents also find that signing opens a window into their child's mind that profoundly enriches the experience of parenting.

In the following story, the Baby Signs program helped turn one sleepless night into a sublime experience of sharing for a father long before his son had the ability to speak.

Thirteen-month-old Bryce often had difficulty sleeping through the night. One morning just before dawn, he awoke and began to cry. Realizing it was his turn, Bryce's dad, Norm, reluctantly crawled out of bed and went in to comfort Bryce—typically not an easy job. Norm thought a change of scenery might help them both, so he took Bryce out on the front porch, sat down on the glider, and began to glide back and forth. Just as they were settling in, Bryce noticed the sun peeking up from the horizon. Still whimpering, he looked at his dad with tear-stained cheeks and flashed his fingers, making the sign for light. *Norm's heart melted, and he hugged*

Bryce tightly. "That's right, Brycie. The sun is coming up and giving us its light." Norm still remembers this as one of his favorite moments with his son.

Let's consider what young Sophia, Jennifer, and Bryce have in common. In each case a baby was able to convey a message without words and enjoy the experience of being quickly and accurately understood. Interchanges such as these foster feelings of competence and trust, and mitigate frustration. The result is a warmer, more satisfying relationship between child and adult. It's a basic fact of human life that when we can communicate with others, we feel more connected. And when that connection, especially between parent and child, yields lots of positive interactions—such as those experienced by these three children—the product is almost inevitably deep feelings of affection and love.

Our research has found that using signs decreases tears and tantrums. The reason is not hard to understand. Unsuccessful communication is often the reason for meltdowns during the "terrible twos" (a period of time that can actually start in the first year and extend into the third). When babies and toddlers are able to communicate their needs, they are much less likely to resort to moaning, crying, and frustrated tantrums to

The Baby Signs Program in Action

This Little Piggy Went to Market
Fifteen-month-old Brandon was so enchanted with a potbelly pig at a street fair in a neighboring town that he used his sign for *pig* to let his parents know he wanted to see it again . . . and again . . . and again. His parents happily obliged, enjoying the fact that he could actually tell them what he wanted. But something even more amazing happened six weeks later on a second visit to the town. Despite the complete absence of the fair and pig, Brandon suddenly began to sign *pig* with great glee. At first his parents were confused, but then they realized they were standing in the exact spot where the pig had been six weeks earlier! Not only had he remembered a pig seen long ago, but he had also remembered the exact grassy spot by the sidewalk where it had been. His parents were amazed!

express themselves. No doubt this is partly the reason we found in our research that using the Baby Signs program actually makes family life easier and strengthens a baby's bond with parents, siblings, grandparents, and caregivers.

Benefit 2: Allows You to See How Smart Your Baby Is

Not only is the inability of babies to communicate very frustrating to parents, it also leads them to assume that their babies are not thinking about things, are not aware of what is happening around them. As we describe in our second book, *Baby Minds*, an enormous amount of cognitive activity is actually going on in their little heads, even at birth. Certainly, by the time they are nine to twelve months old, babies are simply bursting with things to talk about, but they generally have to wait until eighteen months to two years for the words that enable them to do so. That's why, once they start using signs with their children, parents are amazed at how much their babies notice, understand, and remember about the world.

The three real-life stories we have described provide good examples of how much smarter babies are than we often assume. Sophia, Jennifer, and Bryce may not have been talking yet, but they knew quite well what they wanted to say, and with the Baby Signs program they could say it. At the same time, those around them got a wonderful glimpse into just how much was going on in their heads. Sophia was able to tell her mom she had a fever, Jennifer was able to demonstrate an impressive grasp of the animal kingdom, and Bryce was able to help his father appreciate the specialness of an otherwise frustrating moment. Unlike most parents, who have to guess what their babies are thinking, the parents of Sophia, Jennifer, and Bryce could easily follow their children's lead, focusing attention where the babies most needed it to be. With a window into their baby's mind they otherwise would not have, parents of signing babies learn a valuable lesson: there truly is "somebody home in there."

Benefit 3: Helps Your Baby Speak Sooner

It's easy to understand how using signs reduces frustration. One of the other well-established benefits, however, may surprise you. Babies taught signs actually learn to speak sooner and have richer vocabularies. In one of our studies, the signing babies on average knew about fifty more real words than their non-signing peers by the age of two. Moreover, these gains did not disappear as time went on. A year later, at age three, the signers were both saying and understanding words at levels almost comparable to what is expected at age four! Why does the Baby Signs program help babies master language more quickly? Here are a few possible explanations:

- **Food for thought for the brain.**
  Babies come into this world with a mind-boggling 100 to 200 billion brain cells (or neurons). What they don't come into the world with are the trillions and trillions of connections among these neurons. These connections, as much as the neurons themselves, are what enable them to organize thoughts, see relationships among things, remember past events, and master language. How do these connections come about? Both their creation and their continued existence depend a great deal on a child's experiences in the world. The more often a child encounters thought-

provoking objects, events, and problems, the more connections are made and strengthened.

This general principle is clearly relevant to the relation between signing and learning to talk. Every time a baby successfully uses a sign, changes occur in the brain, bringing the child closer to mastering language. The circuitry in the brain—which talking requires—develops along with a child's experience with language. Because using signs enables children to begin the process earlier, the development of this circuitry gets a significant jump start that continues to pay off for years down the road.

- **Like crawling is to walking.**
  Just as babies learn to crawl before they can walk, using signs gives them a developmentally appropriate way to communicate before they can talk. Once children learn to walk, they no longer crawl because of the greater freedom walking affords them. Communication is the same way. While signs are useful before children have words, speech allows them the ability to communicate more quickly and more fully. As your child's mind and body develop, she will naturally transition to speaking in order to convey ever more complex ideas and longer sentences. Far from getting in the way of the process, using the Baby Signs program provides a bridge that helps the transition from no language to spoken language.

- **A tutorial for talking.**
  The experience of signing teaches babies useful lessons about how language works—lessons that speed up the process of learning to talk once words are finally available. By enabling a baby to practice learning and using symbols to label objects, express needs, and describe feelings, signing creates the mental framework that makes it easy to incorporate words as soon as the baby's vocal chords are developed enough to use them.

- **A richer speech environment.**

  The natural reaction to a baby's use of a sign is to "bathe" the child with words, and the more words a child hears, the faster she will learn to talk. Using the Baby Signs program results in children hearing lots of words and sentences directly relevant to the topic they have chosen. We always encourage parents to say the word every time that they or their baby use a sign. Not only will you be using words right along with any signs you show your child, but once he begins to produce signs on his own, you will find yourself responding with words and words and more words. When she begins to look at you and sniff for *flowers* while strolling through the park, you will automatically respond with something like, "Oh, you see the flowers! Yes, those are pretty flowers. We see lots of flowers, don't we?" This exposure to words they care about is exactly what children need in order to learn how to say the words themselves.

  The three examples we've included in this chapter, the stories of Sophia, Jennifer, and Bryce, illustrate some of these factors underlying the positive effects of signing on verbal language. In each case, the use of the Baby Signs program provided the children with exactly the kind of rich

---

Benefits in Brief

Our research studies, funded by the National Institutes of Health, have revealed numerous benefits for babies and for families. Using the Baby Signs program

- reduces tears, tantrums, and frustration;
- allows babies to express their needs and share their worlds;
- enriches daily interactions and strengthens the parent-child bond;
- reveals how smart babies truly are by providing parents a window into their baby's mind;
- helps babies develop language skills and speak sooner;
- builds a positive foundation for a baby's future emotional development by helping her express her feelings in a constructive way;
- jump-starts intellectual development, resulting in higher IQs in elementary school; and
- boosts a baby's self-esteem and self-confidence.

interpersonal conversation that yields faster language development. Our research files are filled with experiences like these. When combined with the objective data we obtained from over a dozen standardized language tests, they enable us to sum up our two decades of research on language development in one short statement: we now can say conclusively that encouraging babies to use signs not only leads to better communication before words come along, but it also makes learning to talk easier. (For more details about the transition to speech, please see Chapter 6.)

Benefit 4: Jump-Starts Intellectual and Emotional Growth

Learning to talk is only one of the cognitive benefits of the Baby Signs program. Our research suggests that using signs also has significant and long-term benefits for your child's growing brain. The signing babies in our study, who had greater language skills than their nonsigning peers, also scored more impressively on tests of mental development, pretend play, and the ability to remember where things are. We wondered, however, what the effects of the Baby Signs program, especially its positive effect on learning to talk, would be down the line.

At the urging of those parents in our research studies who suspected that there were long-term benefits, we conducted a follow-up to our National Institutes of Health study. We compared two groups of eight-year-olds, former signers and nonsigners, using the WISC-III, a traditional IQ test. The results were startling and impressive. The children who had been signers had IQ scores on the average 12 points higher than their nonsigning peers. They scored an average of 114, while the children who had never learned signs averaged 102. (The average child in the United States scores 100 on the test.) We controlled for family income, education, and other factors that influence IQ scores. What does this mean? While the nonsigners were on average scoring just about as you would expect eight-year-olds to score, the former signers were performing more like nine-year-olds! (For details of this follow-up study, see Appendix B.)

Why such a positive long-term effect? For one thing, we believe that the early language advantage that signing yields serves children very well as they continue on into elementary school, helping them understand things better, explain things better, and ask better questions when they are confused. This possibility is strongly supported by independent research from Stanford University by Virginia Marchman and Anne Fernald showing that babies with better verbal language skills at twenty-five months did significantly better on cognitive tests at eight years. They suggest that improvements in what researchers call *working memory* (the ability to hold things in immediate memory) may be what underlies the connection.

It also seems likely that the love of books we see develop among signing babies—because they can take an active role in labeling things very early on—continues to stand them in good stead as they learn to read. Given that reading is fundamental to achievement in school, anything that supports the development of literacy is likely to also promote advanced cognitive skills.

On the emotional side, as a result of being able to communicate effectively from the moment they feel they need to, we suspect that signing babies develop a "can-do" attitude. Evidence for this positive effect on self-confidence comes not only from our own observations, but also from parents of signers who consistently report that their children seem proud of themselves when they succeed in communicating what's on their minds. Earlier than they would otherwise, signers begin to conceive of themselves as genuine players in the business of the family—real conversational partners whose observations and concerns truly matter. They may be little, but because of the Baby Signs program, they no longer need to feel quite so frustrated and powerless.

In fact, the pride and self-esteem that come from feeling heard and understood may have significant long-term emotional benefits. The scientific community is learning more and more each day about the enormous importance of emotional development during the first three years. (This is the subject of our third book, *Baby Hearts*—see Appendix D for more information on this resource.) It is during these three crucial years that babies learn what to expect from the world and how the world responds to them. The importance of their being able to communicate their needs, joys, and fears during this critical time—and have them understood—should not be underestimated. This is why we truly believe that what the Baby Signs program can do for a baby's heart matters even more than what it does for her mind.

Whether or not these explanations totally account for the long-term positive effects of signing uncovered in our research, the bottom line remains the same. The evidence is overwhelming that the Baby Signs experience provides children with a head start that continues to benefit them long after they've left the world of signing for the wider world of words.

As Easy as Waving Bye-Bye

Our goal for this book is to help you and your baby learn to sign so that, like hundreds of thousands of other families, you can enjoy the many benefits we've described. Just as Sophia, Jennifer, and Bryce have done, your baby can easily learn simple signs for objects, events, feelings, and needs. With these signs literally at your baby's fingertips, communication between you can flourish during that difficult time from about six to thirty months, when your baby's desire to communicate outstrips his capacity to say words. By increasing the number of signs in your baby's repertoire, the two of you can "talk" about lots more things than your baby's few early words would permit.

And why are we so sure your baby can do it? The answer is simple: in a lifetime of observing babies, as well as two decades of research on the Baby Signs program, we haven't yet met a baby who couldn't—and neither have you! Think of babies waving bye-bye and shaking their heads. Or think of babies singing "Eensy-Weensy Spider" accompanied by the signs for *spider*, *rain*, and *sun*.

These are all signs, just like Sophia blowing for *hot*, Bryce flashing his fingers for *light*, and Jennifer bouncing up and down for *kangaroo*. All are simply signs with specific meanings that children can use to talk about things in their world before they have words.

In their eagerness to join the social world around them, babies pick up the signs for *bye-bye*, *yes*, and *no* easily. With this book you will learn how easy it is to take this natural tendency a step further and open up an exciting channel of communication between you and your child. *Bye-bye* may be the first sign your baby learns, but it certainly need not be the last. By adding signs to her fledgling attempts to talk, you can help your baby express needs, learn about the world, and, best of all, forge bonds of affection and satisfaction with you and other loved ones that can last a lifetime.

CHAPTER 2

The Baby Signs Program:
Right for Every Family

Some parents insist on teaching their babies authentic ASL signs, shunning... nonstandard signs; others don't consider the distinction important. Some are using the signs only as a temporary bridge to speech; others want their children to become bilingual. Personal preference plays a major role....Babies are [just] delighted to be able to share their feelings, desires, questions and curiosity with others, knowing that others understand them.

—Matthew Moore, *Deaf Life*, March 2007

(Full article available at www.babysigns.com)

OUR SCIENTIFIC RESEARCH, PERSONAL OBSERVATIONS, AND common sense all tell us that babies desperately want to be "heard." So eager are they to connect with people in their lives that when they are given the opportunity to learn signs, they enthusiastically accept this nonverbal means of "talking." Babies don't care which signs parents choose to teach them; they will accept any sign that helps them be understood.

In contrast, some parents have firm opinions on this score. Some parents prefer teaching their babies only ASL signs, and there are many reasons to use this approach. Other families want the flexibility to use non-ASL signs, and there are just as many reasons to use this approach. Both strategies work well for babies. So, which approach should you choose? The signs you choose to use with your baby should be based on what you and your family are most comfortable using, your goals for signing with your baby, and, most of all, what works best for both of you. Your goal is the same in either case and is the same as ours—to help your baby reap all the benefits of the Baby Signs program.

The remainder of this chapter is dedicated to helping you make the best choice for your family between these two strategies. But keep in mind that even after you settle on a strategy you are free to change it. Some parents start with an all-ASL approach but find it doesn't work for them as well as they expected. If this happens to you, don't stop signing with your baby. Just adopt a more flexible approach. Some families start with the more flexible approach and become so intrigued with signing that they want to explore ASL further. These families just shift to more exact ASL and keep signing. Again, babies don't care—as long as you give them signs that they can use until they can talk!

The Baby Signs All-ASL Program

American Sign Language (ASL) is the official language of the Deaf community in the United States. The roots of ASL, according to most scholars, can be traced back to the early 1800s, when Thomas Hopkins Gallaudet decided to dedicate his life to educating deaf children in America. In 1816, Gallaudet, along with his French colleague Laurent Clerc, established the first public school for the Deaf in America, introducing students to French Sign Language (FSL).

But, just as babies in their desperation to communicate will spontaneously create their own signs, so, too, had Deaf communities in various parts of the country created their own indigenous signing systems. Gradually, the signs and rules of these informal sign languages became intertwined with the more established formal FSL. The resulting system is what we now call American Sign Language (ASL), a fully functioning language every bit as complex as any spoken language, with thousands of precise signs and complex rules of grammar.

Like spoken English, ASL is a continuously evolving language that tolerates flexibility to a greater extent than many people realize. Variations in the specific forms of signs abound in formal sign languages, not just across international boundaries, but even within countries. For example, *Signs Across America* (Gallaudet College Press) documents twelve different ASL signs for *cereal*, thirteen different ASL signs for *cake*, and fourteen different ASL signs for *candy* in the United States alone!

> Like other languages, ASL is continuously evolving. The result is a great deal of variability from area to area—and dictionary to dictionary—in the form that signs take, a fact that comes as a surprise to many people outside the Deaf community.

With this variation in mind, we worked in consultation with Jamie Stevens, ASL interpreter for the Deaf, and under the guidance of the ASL department at Columbia College, Chicago, to determine for each ASL sign included in Appendix C the form that is most commonly used today within the United States. The resulting Baby Signs ASL dictionary now includes ASL signs for 150 of the things babies most want and need to communicate about during their first two to three years—like signs for mealtime, bedtime, bathtime, feelings, animals, and many others. But the list is not exhaustive, and finding signs for your unique experiences may require looking further. When you need a sign that is not included in the dictionary, there are many good ASL dictionaries and websites you can turn to. We've provided references to some of the most useful of these at the end of Appendix B.

Is an All-ASL Approach Right for Your Family?

Parents who use an all-ASL approach do so for a variety of reasons. To determine whether this is the best approach for your family, ask yourself the following questions:

1. **Do you have a Deaf family member or friend?** If so, an all-ASL approach will be worth your efforts, whether you already use ASL yourself or you want to learn it to be able to communicate with your friend or family member. Not only will you be helping your hearing baby communicate with you, but you will also be helping him build a communication bridge to the Deaf people in his life.

2. **Do you already know ASL, or are you interested in learning it?** If you already know ASL, then it makes sense to go with what you know. If you don't already know ASL but would like to learn it, this is a great time to start. Because you will be teaching only simple signs to your baby, there is no need for you to learn ASL word order or rules of use before using it with your baby. Learning along with your baby is a good way to start out slowly and yet quickly experience success.

3. **Do you want to introduce your child to ASL as a second language?** Many parents see signing with their babies as an opportunity to teach them a second language. Whether it's Spanish, French, or ASL, exposing babies to different languages can be very beneficial to their overall language development. However, in order for anyone, babies included, to learn a language, they must hear it (or see it, in the case of ASL) regularly. If your child is not exposed to fluent ASL users, she will not learn it as a second language simply from learning signs. So, if you are fluent

in ASL or your baby spends lots of time with someone who is, then this is an excellent opportunity for your baby.

4. **Is it important to you that the signs you teach your baby be consistent with those used by other families or childcare providers?**
Many parents tell us that they want to use only ASL signs so that their child's signs will be consistent with those he sees in childcare environments. As signing with hearing babies has become more and more mainstream, many childcare centers have incorporated signing into their infant and toddler classrooms. Some centers adopt an all-ASL approach, but many others use a more flexible, baby-friendly approach. If this is an issue for you, check with your childcare center about whether they use signing with the babies and toddlers in their care and which signs they are using.

Keep in mind, however, that ASL signs vary from area to area, and just because a center has chosen to use ASL signs does not guarantee that every sign will be exactly the same as the ASL sign you are using. The good news is that caregivers and babies easily work out differences

> **The Baby Signs Program in Action**
>
> **Bridging the Gap**
> Sixteen-month-old Chloe and her mother were sitting on a bench at the California State Fair when a family of four sat down on a bench next to them and began signing to one another in an animated fashion. Chloe, a veteran student of the Baby Signs program with two dozen signs of her own, began watching them very closely. Just then, the father of the foursome pulled a balloon out of his pocket, blew it up, and quickly twisted it into a funny-looking creature. That was all Chloe needed to see. Before her mother knew it, Chloe had hopped down and toddled the short distance to the other bench—where she began signing with eyes wide, *balloon please, Balloon Please, BALLOON PLEASE!* The father, needless to say, was delighted to comply, especially after Chloe's mom explained to the one member of the family who was not deaf that Chloe was indeed an avid signer herself!

between signs just as they do differences between words. For example, the word for *cat* might be "ki-ki" for one child and "ti-ti" for another. Caregivers quickly understand each baby's idiosyncrasies in terms of both words and signs.

If you have answered yes to one or more of these questions, then an all-ASL approach should work well for your family. However, if you are new to ASL, we would like to call your attention to a few things that you might want to watch for regarding your baby's progress.

1. Exact ASL includes some "lexicalized" signs that require "fingerspelling" words—even words for simple things babies like to talk about, like *bus* and *bubbles*. If you are experienced with ASL, you will know how to use a "classifier" for the lexicalized signs that call for them. If you are new to ASL, you might want to use the baby-friendly alternative in these few

What's Most Important Is That It Works!

Q: *My child is using a different sign than the one I'm teaching him. I have been tapping my fingertips together as a sign for* more, *and my baby still just taps his two fists together. He doesn't seem to be making any progress toward using his fingers. What should I do?*

A: Many parents have expressed a similar concern. Our advice is to give him lots of recognition for what he is doing. Remember that the main goal of the Baby Signs program is to help the two of you understand each other. If your baby's signs only approximate what you have been showing him, that's OK. As long as you each know what the other is "saying," the Baby Signs program is working. As his motor abilities improve, so will the accuracy of his signs.

situations. Remember, even the strongest ASL advocates tolerate some variations and modifications.

2. Although your baby may be able to comprehend even complex ASL signs, some complex signs will simply be beyond her physical ability to produce accurately. Still, she may give it a try, the result being only a vague approximation of the sign. This is very similar to what babies do with words. Sign and word approximations can be difficult for adults to decipher, so watch carefully for these subtle attempts and reinforce her efforts. Just as babies' words become more and more intelligible as their articulation improves, so, too, will her signs become more discernible as her motor skills become more refined.

3. Be aware of those signs you are using regularly that your baby is not even attempting. It may be that the sign is just too complex for her to grasp. Again, a similar situation occurs with spoken words. Research shows that children's choice of first words is influenced by the unique combination of sounds that make up a word. Even though they can produce the individual sounds, when the combination of sounds is too complex, children simply don't try to say the words—even though these are words they hear many times a day for objects that are very relevant to their lives. Take, for example, the word *diaper*. It is not among children's early words. Even though they clearly understand the meaning of the word (ask them to get you a diaper and they know exactly what to do), they make no attempt to say it until their language skills are better developed.

    Watch for similar situations with ASL signs. If you find that your baby is not attempting a sign that you are regularly using with her, it might be because its complexity is beyond her ability. Try offering her a simplified version as a temporary bridge to help her communicate until she can physically master the exact ASL version.

4. *Always* use the spoken word along with the sign. Since true ASL does not follow the word order or grammatical rules of spoken English, it typically is not accompanied by spoken words. However, for hearing babies, signing is simply a temporary bridge to talking—and for babies to learn to talk they must hear lots of words. Even if your goal is to continue signing with your baby in order to teach him ASL as a second language, it is still critical for him to hear the words along with the signs. The Baby Signs program is not meant to promote signing instead of talking. If your two-year-old is signing away but is not yet very vocal, make sure you are always providing him with lots of opportunities to hear spoken language.

> Hearing children need to hear lots of words in order to learn to talk. That's why the Baby Signs program emphasizes always using signs and words together even if parents are using an all-ASL approach.

In summary, if you choose to use an all-ASL approach, you and your baby will experience many great benefits: you will be exposing your baby to a rich and vital language, you will be expanding your own horizons, and you may even be launching a new adventure in learning a second language. We wish you lots of success!

The Baby Signs "Baby-Friendly" Program

We encourage ASL use, but we want to avoid sending the message that all parents *must* use ASL signs or they are doing something wrong. Because we know how beneficial it is for hearing babies to communicate with signs, we don't want to put any obstacles in the paths of their parents. For example, this flexibility allays the fears of parents who are worried by the need to adhere to a precise system with which they are unfamiliar or who, when they hear that a program requires ASL signs, interpret the message (mistakenly) to mean they have to learn a whole new language. It is to reassure parents like these that the Baby Signs program also offers an alternative, more flexible approach based on the philosophy that effective communication between parent and baby—not the specific form of the signs used to achieve it—is what counts.

Baby-Friendly Signs

Baby-friendly signs include alternatives to exact ASL signs that may be easier for young babies to make. They include both slightly modified ASL signs and some signs that are completely different. By slightly modifying some ASL signs, our goal is to give babies some simplified versions that may provide them with more opportunities to successfully use the sign. For example, take the sign for *duck*. The ASL sign is made by holding the back of your hand to your mouth and tapping your thumb to your index and middle finger. The baby-friendly, modified version is done by simply putting your hand out and making a quacking motion. Since many parents, whether signing or not, use this hand motion when talking about ducks with their babies, it is both easy to do and easy to remember.

Baby-friendly signs also include some that have no relationship to ASL. These include the signs that babies in our research studies spontaneously created. Since we know that babies can easily do these signs (because they came from the babies themselves), we include these for your use. These include signs for *bird, fish, dog, flower, pig*, and many more.

> The signs that babies create themselves often involve large muscle movements within their faces, heads, and whole bodies rather than their fingers because control of the fine motor movements of their fingers develops much later.

Baby-friendly signs take advantage of a baby's natural progression of motor skills development, thereby making it easier for little hands to master the signs they need to get their messages across. As your newborn grew into a six-month-old, she gained greater control over her body. First she could lift her head, then her shoulders, then her torso. This natural progression of directional development is what is known as *cephalocaudal development*, literally development from the head to the tail. A second directional principle of physical development is known as *proximodistal development*—from the close to the distant—and explains why a baby's physical control proceeds from the center of her body outward to her extremities, first to her shoulders, then to her arms, then to her hands, and finally to her fingers. Because control of hands and fingers occurs so much later, baby-friendly signs often involve the use of a baby's face (especially the mouth), head, and whole body in the form of gross motor (rather than fine motor) movements. It is because of our knowledge of these natural developmental limitations that we believe it is important to offer families baby-friendly alternatives to especially complex ASL signs, alternatives that take advantage of babies' physical assets rather than rely on their physical limitations.

The Baby Signs dictionary includes photo illustrations and written descriptions of thirty-five baby-friendly alternatives to exact ASL signs. Those parents who like this more flexible approach can use as many ASL signs as they want and still choose baby-friendly alternatives whenever they think it will be helpful to their baby.

Is a Flexible Approach Right for Your Family?

To help you decide whether to include baby-friendly signs and your own baby's creations in your signing repertoire, consider the following reasons other families have told us they like this flexibility.

1. Flexibility allows parents to adapt signs to their own baby's abilities, making it easier for them to experience success as early as possible. A common adaptation that many parents use is one for *big*. The ASL sign is made by holding the index fingers and thumbs out (both hands forming the L hand shape) and moving the hands apart. Instead of using the L hand shape, parents simply use their open palms. This adaptation makes the sign easier for their babies to learn and remember.

2. Flexibility allows for signs that are completely different from ASL but more closely related to babies' own experiences—something that a baby is more likely to notice. Take, for example, the ASL sign for *cereal*. One ASL version mimics eating cereal from a bowl. Although easy enough for babies to do, it does not relate to their actual experience of eating cereal, which is typically picking up Cheerios with their fingers. Although it is not necessary for signs to relate to the concepts they represent, a relationship, whether in form or in function, can be a strong reminder for both baby and parent alike.

3. Flexibility allows parents to include signs from the songs and games their baby may already be learning—like those involved in "Eensy-Weensy Spider" and "Little Bunny Foo Foo." Singing songs and playing games involving specific gestures can be confusing for babies if they are simultaneously being taught different ASL signs for the same objects.

Adopting the baby-friendly signs from such games and songs—like rubbing index fingers together for *spider* and making a V-hand shape for *bunny*—makes it both simple and easy for babies to learn the signs. And these signs work equally well to name pictures and label real spiders and bunnies as they do within the songs.

4. Flexibility allows parents to take advantage of unexpected teaching moments—such as surprise encounters with caterpillars at the park or helicopters in the sky. A flexible approach means that parents can make the most of their child's fascination by creating signs "on the fly," so to speak, rather than having to wait until they can access an ASL dictionary hoping to find a precise ASL sign. Why is this important? Many parents report that their children have used such signs to talk about the experience hours, days, and even months later. What a shame it would have been, they say, to miss such precious opportunities simply because they didn't know the "right" sign.

5. Flexibility allows parents to use any signs that their babies create—and many babies do create signs. In the early days of our research, we discovered this is true of babies who

> **The Baby Signs Program in Action**
>
> **A Marshmallow by Any Other Name Is Still a Marshmallow**
> Emma, a full-fledged signer at fourteen months, was used to being shown a sign for the things she needed to "talk" about. But when she and her mom, Amy, passed the marshmallows on the shelf in the grocery store and Emma looked to Amy as if asking for the sign, Amy was stumped. She didn't know the *marshmallow* sign and was at a loss for how to respond to Emma's persistent requests. As Amy readily admits, her creative mind was evidently asleep, because all she could think of was to pat the back of her left arm with her right hand. This sign in no way related to a marshmallow, but it didn't matter a bit to Emma. She gave Amy a smile of satisfaction and began to use her new sign—which, by the way, continued to work just fine for several months until Emma could say *marshmallow*.

are not being taught signs by their parents. In their desperation to communicate, they recruit physical movements that are associated with the object they are eager to talk about—like panting for *dog* and sniffing for *flower*. Now we know that it is equally true of children whose parents *are* teaching them signs. It's as if, once babies learn that signing is a great way to get what they need or call Mom and Dad's attention to something interesting, they become

> A parent's use of signs often leads babies to create signs of their own because they recognize that their parent is open to this channel of communication.

enthusiastic sign creators to speed the process along. Acknowledging such creations provides parents with a wonderful opportunity to do what researchers find, in general, best promotes learning—follow their child's lead rather than compelling the child to follow theirs. In addition, the simple act of exercising creative skills is a great way for babies to boost brain power and foster positive self-esteem!

In summary, if you choose this more flexible approach, you can rest assured that you will be providing your baby just as solid a foundation for learning to talk as parents who opt for an all-ASL strategy. And remember, if you decide to carry on signing with your child beyond the point at which she no longer needs signs, you can always transition to exact ASL signs once she has developed better control of her hands. Just as she will move on from using baby words like *tummy* and *Mommy* to adult words like *stomach* and *Mom* once her ability to articulate improves, she can easily move on from baby-friendly signs to ASL. In other words, just because your baby uses a less common form of a sign at age one doesn't mean she can't easily learn a different form of the sign at age two or three when her little hands are better able to produce it.

More About Baby Creations

We are absolutely convinced that most babies, in their eagerness to communicate, create signs. Being alert to such signs is especially important once your baby has become accustomed to using signs. In fact, your own use of signs is a green light signaling to your baby your openness to this channel of communication. With this realization, your baby is quite likely to experiment with some of his own. The trick is to know what to look for.

Watch for unusual actions that your baby seems to do repeatedly and with a determined air, simple actions linked in time with things around him. Often, but not always, these will be accompanied by a look to you, as if to check to see if you have understood.

Babies are remarkably acute observers of objects on their own. They notice what things look like and what they do, then figure out how to convey both characteristics through sign, even without your demonstrating. Some babies we have studied have noticed, all on their own, that dogs pant, that balls roll, that wind moves things back and forth, that hats cover heads, that Christmas lights blink on and off, and that swings move back and forth. In each case, the baby spontaneously turned the characteristic into a sign. Fortunately for these babies, their parents were smart enough to figure out what was going on.

Seventeen-month-old Brandon provides a particularly endearing example of baby creativity. Brandon's parents and grandparents had been teaching him signs since he was nine months old. With their help, he learned *kitty*, *doggie*, *more*, and lots of others that served him well. However, no one had thought to provide him with a sign for one of his favorite objects, the camera. Why camera? Brandon was not only a first child, but also a first grandchild. With all the picture-taking that had gone on in his short life, he had seen cameras of one kind or another almost as frequently as he had his bottle. The camera, in other words, was clearly a significant object in his daily life. So, it shouldn't have been surprising at all when one day Brandon curled his right hand into an arch, lifted it to eye level, and squinted with one eye through the "hole" it formed. It was such an accurate portrait of a camera that there was no mystery about what he wanted. He had invented his own *camera* sign!

Like Brandon, your baby might surprise you by coming up with a sign or two on her own. Just be open, observant, and enthusiastic. If you do notice such a sign, your supportive response will automatically boost your baby's confidence in her power to communicate and will spur the whole language enterprise. It also, of course, gains you a few early points with her as a sensitive and insightful parent.

A Program for Everyone

Our goal with this chapter has been to alert you to the options now available within the Baby Signs program. Although in its earliest form the program focused on signs created by the parents and babies who participated in our research studies, that is no longer the case. As more and more parents joined the movement, we began to recognize the opportunity we had to build a bridge to the Deaf community. With that in mind, we incorporated many ASL signs into our 2002 edition of *Baby Signs*, and now, in this edition, we are completing the progression with an all-ASL approach. At the same time, however, we are presenting the "best of both worlds" by also including guidance for a more flexible strategy that welcomes whatever signs parents or babies feel work best for them. As we hope we've made clear in the chapter, both approaches have much to recommend them, and whichever one you choose, you can be sure that your baby will be thrilled by your efforts to open a channel of communication between you—no matter what form the signs take.

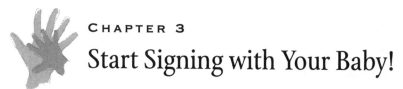

CHAPTER 3

Start Signing with Your Baby!

When I first heard about the Baby Signs program, I thought, "But I know nothing about sign language." Much to my surprise and pleasure, the more I learned about it, the more I realized that I was practically doing it already without even knowing it. It comes so easily!

—Mother of sixteen-month-old Anthony

When to Start Signing

Now that you know all about the Baby Signs program, you're probably eager to start signing with your baby. But where do you begin? Your first step is to decide whether you want to try an all-ASL approach or include some baby-friendly alternatives when you begin signing with your baby. Remember that your decision is not set in stone. It's easy to change your approach any time along the way if it is not working as easily or as quickly as you had hoped. The goal is communication, and what matters most is what works best for you and your baby.

The purpose of this chapter is to give you the information you need to help your family have the most successful and rewarding signing experience possible. We will help you determine when your baby is ready to start signing and which signs are best to begin with. We will provide you with some teaching strategies to make learning easy, fun, and successful. And we will give you some ways to evaluate your baby's progress.

Is Your Baby Ready for Signs?

The question of when to begin is by far the one we hear most frequently from parents. There is no specific age at which we can say all babies will be ready to sign. Every baby sets her own timetable based on her specific interests, experiences, and rate of development. Some babies put learning to crawl, walk, and climb at the top of their priority list, while other babies prefer learning to stack blocks and manipulate toys. Still others are keenly interested in people and spend large amounts of time and energy trying to get their attention. Based on our research, we can say that most babies develop an interest in signing between nine and twelve months. However, we strongly advise parents not to focus exclusively on the age of their baby. Much more important is to watch for your baby to develop an interest in communicating. For some babies, this point comes earlier than nine months; for others it comes later than twelve months. Whatever your baby's age, an interest in communicating is a good sign that she is both willing and able to begin benefiting from the Baby Signs program.

> While the typical age at which babies develop an interest in signing is between nine and twelve months, it's important to watch for your baby's interest in communicating.

How Will I Know When My Baby Wants to Communicate?

One of the most striking indications that communicating has become a priority for your baby is an increased interest in people and things, and especially in using the first (people) to find out about the second (things). Your baby will begin to point to things more than he has before, and his pointing may be accompanied by "Uh, uh!" as if asking, "What's that?"

For example, when you go to the park, you may find that he points to the slide, the swing, or a baby in a stroller. And, if you are like most parents, you will happily provide the name for each.

When to Start Teaching Signs

Q:*When should I start signing? Is six months too young?*

A: You can start signing the day your baby is born. However, many parents find it more convenient to start closer to the time when their baby is showing interest in communicating. How can you tell? If your answer is yes to any of the following questions, now is a good time to start.

- Is your baby at least six months old?
- Is your baby beginning to point to things?
- Is your baby bringing toys or objects to you and looking for a response?
- Is your baby beginning to wave *bye-bye*?
- Is your baby beginning to shake his head *no* or *yes*?
- Is your baby beginning to take an interest in picture books?
- Is your baby frustrated when you don't understand what she needs?
- Are there still important things your baby doesn't have words for?

Besides pointing to things, your baby is likely to show her interest in communicating by bringing toys and other objects to you, holding them out for you to see as if requesting a label. Her eyes will try to catch yours, and she will seem to insist that you acknowledge her effort in some way. Again, you will find yourself quite naturally naming the item. "Oh! A ball!" A broad smile is likely to be your reward.

A third signal that it's time to start introducing signs is an increased interest in picture books. As they approach their first birthday, instead of focusing on tearing the pages out, babies begin to focus their attention on looking at the pictures on each page. They may point to a specific picture, something particularly colorful or familiar, while looking up quizzically as if asking for information. Parents typically respond to this new interest in books by pointing to various pictures themselves and asking, "What's that?" At this early stage parents instinctively know to provide the label themselves, realizing that their baby is not yet capable of producing the answer. "It's a doggie! Doggies say woof-woof!" These exchanges all have something in common. They all are clear indications that your baby is now interested in learning the names of things—and ready to begin learning signs.

As we will explain in greater detail in the next section, the process itself is easy, and the keys to success are clarity, simplicity, and repetition. Whenever your natural inclination is to name the item your baby is interested in, simply show him the sign while you say the word. When he hands you a ball, say clearly and carefully "ball!" and make the *ball* sign. As you do this time after time, your child will begin to understand that the word and the sign both refer to the same thing, that they are equivalent. Once this equivalence is understood, your baby will be better prepared to take the next step—using the sign himself.

When Will My Baby Begin Signing to Me?

Just because your baby sees you using signs doesn't mean she has yet developed the skills and knowledge necessary to do them herself. Think about what babies need before they can spontaneously point at a dog and produce the *dog* sign. As mentioned previously, they need to have seen you do the sign often enough to understand the equivalence between the sign and the object. They also need to be able to imitate the movements involved. Finally, they have to have the memory capacity to recall all these things the moment they see the dog and decide it's important enough to tell you about. Each of these is an important piece of the language puzzle. One wouldn't expect a three-month-old, for example, to fit all these components together. But by the time they are nine to twelve months old, most babies can.

One clear indication that your baby is ready to start using signs himself is the milestone of learning to wave *bye-bye*. Parents almost instinctively teach their children this sign, saying the words and waving their hands. Most don't think of this as a sign, but it really is. It's a simple sign that stands for a concept—somebody or something leaving. Similarly, if your baby is shaking his head for *no* and nodding for *yes*, he's definitely ready to start signing.

Is It Ever Too Early to Begin Teaching Signs?

When parents read about the Baby Signs program, they often want to start right away. Many ask us how early they can start signing to their baby, not wanting to waste a minute. We always tell them that they can start as early as they want; it really doesn't matter. After all, parents start talking to their babies the day they are born (and sometimes even before). The important thing is not to expect them to talk or sign back until all pieces of the puzzle are in place. This means that the earlier you start using signs, the longer you will need to wait before your baby is able to use them herself. Because it's easy to get discouraged if your baby doesn't start signing right away, we generally encourage parents to wait until they see the changes we list in the Q&A box on page 33 indicating that their child is really interested in communicating.

Sometimes it's just as important to recognize that the parent is ready even if the baby isn't. If this is the case, we say go for it! Just as there is no harm in talking to your baby before she is ready to talk, using signs before she is ready to sign will certainly not hurt her if you are willing to be patient. It's really OK to start when you feel ready. Start with just a few signs, and keep in mind that for all babies the first signs take the longest. Should your baby need a little more time to catch on, be prepared to wait—you'll be planting the seeds of communication and soon be reaping the rewards of understanding.

The ABCDs of the Baby Signs Program

Here are four easy tips to keep in mind when teaching signs:

- **A**lways say the word when you make the sign.
- **B**e patient. The younger the child, the longer it takes to learn a sign.
- **C**reate opportunities to use signs; repetition is the key to success.
- **D**o it in a way that makes signing fun and easy for the whole family.

Finally, it is worth mentioning that learning signs, like all aspects of a child's development, is not a race or a competition. While parents understandably take pride in their children's achievements, it is important not to push them or worry whether they are learning or developing "fast enough." All babies develop at their own rate, and just as all babies learn to speak when they are ready, all babies learn to sign when they are ready.

What if My Baby Is Already Using Words? Is It Too Late?

If your baby is older than twelve months or has already begun to use some words, there are still very good reasons to teach him signs. Our research shows that babies can benefit from signing any time during their first two and a half years. Remember that a baby's early vocabulary typically consists of a few simple words and that new words are added very slowly. Words like *crocodile*, *giraffe*, *hippopotamus*, and even *swing* are difficult for babies to say, yet these are things that interest them when on outings to the zoo or the park or when looking at books. They want to "talk" to you about them, but they can't because the words are too long and complicated. The Baby Signs program provides a way for your baby to overcome these obstacles and communicate effectively about a wider variety of things than their words alone would allow. If your baby has already demonstrated his communication readiness, either with or without words, now is a great time to start introducing signs.

How to Get Started: Ten Tips for Success

Teaching your baby to sign is as easy as teaching her to wave *bye-bye* because all that's involved is showing your baby the sign and saying the word, just as you do when you teach your baby to wave *bye-bye*. However, parents often ask for more detailed guidance, so we offer the following ten tips that have helped other families get started.

1. Start with Just a Few

If you are brand new to the Baby Signs program, it's a good idea to pick out just a few signs to start with. (We provide some especially good candidates in Chapter 4.) The reason has more to do with you than with your baby. We find that parents need some time to get used to the idea of signing. Until you get into the habit of using a particular sign whenever an opportunity arises, it's all too easy to forget which signs you are teaching, and this is especially likely if you are trying to teach lots of signs at the same time. Once into the swing of signing, you can judge for yourself how quickly to add new ones to your list. As far as your baby is concerned, the more

> Even when a child has a large spoken vocabulary, she may still use signs for difficult words like *elephant* or *crocodile.*

the merrier. Just as Deaf babies do when surrounded by adults using lots of ASL signs, hearing babies simply choose from signs they see based on which they are able to do and which ones they feel will serve them best.

2. Always Use the Sign and Word Together

Because you are using signs as a bridge to speech, it is important to say the word as you make the sign. Connecting the sign with the word for your child reinforces both. Keep in mind that signing is a way to help your baby "talk" by providing him with a choice. When he hears the word and sees the sign, he has two options available instead of only one. Some words, like *ball* or *up*, will be easier for your baby to say than others. In those cases, he may choose to learn the word right from the beginning. Other words, like *flower*, may be more difficult, and your baby may therefore choose the sign. By using signs and words together, you are leaving both doors open. What's more, even when your baby uses the sign first, he will be learning to understand what you are saying and will have a head start in figuring out how to say the word himself.

3. Repeat the Sign and the Word Several Times

Repetition is the key to learning. The more a baby sees a sign, the easier it is for her to learn it. Emphasize a sign by repeating it several times. When adults talk to babies, their conversations are typically characterized by repetition. For example, when you point to a bird flying up into a tree, you are likely to repeat the word multiple times: "Oh, there's a bird! See the little bird? See the bird up in the tree?" Such repetition helps babies identify exactly which word is the important one, the one that needs to be remembered. Do the same with signs. In these situations use the *bird* sign each time you use the word. Soon your baby will appreciate the special connection between the sign, the word, and the object. She will be on her way to understanding that things in the world have names that can be used to talk about them. Just as with words, you'll find such repetition comes quite naturally.

4. Involve Others

Involving older siblings, grandparents, aunts and uncles, family friends, and caregivers not only helps your baby communicate with these important people, it also gives her many more opportunities for learning. And while dads and grandparents are sometimes hesitant to get on board, once they see how magical signing can be they often become ardent supporters who happily join you in celebrating your baby's signing successes.

5. When Helpful, Gently Guide Your Child's Hands

When it seems helpful, besides simply showing your baby a sign, you can gently manipulate his hands to help him get the feel of the motion. You probably know from your own experience how useful it is to have an expert actually help you form your hands around a golf club or tennis racket as you are learning. You quickly get a sense of how the club or racket should feel in your hands, making it easier next time to do it own your own. Babies are no different. In fact, because they are less experienced, they profit even more than we do from sensitive tactile assistance. But keep in mind that babies can also be pretty independent at times. Some babies like help, while others prefer to do it on their own. Just pay close attention to your baby's response to make sure he likes your help. As is true whatever the situation, awareness of your baby's preferences is most important.

6. Make Signing a Regular Part of Your Day

Signs are a natural outgrowth of how you already interact with your baby. The best way to remember to use signs is to build them into your daily routines: diaper changing, mealtime, bathtime, and bedtime. You can use signs to talk with your baby about anything you are doing.

There are lots of ways to remind you and your baby to sign. For example, hang a picture of a cat above the changing table and talk about the cat using the word and the sign together each time you change your baby's diaper. Choose a special book about dogs for your child's bedtime routine to help you practice the *dog* sign. Use a placemat with birds and a bib decorated with flowers as reminders to teach your baby these signs at each mealtime. If you're working on the *fish* sign, put a fish toy in the bathtub and fish magnets on the refrigerator, and try Goldfish crackers as a snack. When they are gone, ask your baby if she wants *more*. These are all good ways to ensure that your baby gets lots of exposure to the signs you are trying to teach her. Take advantage of whatever toys and pictures you have on hand, and look for ways to incorporate these into enjoyable, easily repeated routines.

In addition to home routines, look for opportunities to use signs on family outings. Label birds at the park, flowers on your neighborhood stroll, toy dogs at the mall, and goldfish in the aquarium at the pediatrician's office. You'll be surprised at how frequently you use signs and how easily they become a part of your daily routines.

7. Use the Sign with Lots of Different Examples

A single word stands for many different things. *Dog* stands for the neighbors' golden retriever as well as the stuffed beagle in the toy store and the picture of the poodle. To truly understand the word (and the concept it represents), a baby has to connect the word to all of these very different-looking things. Similarly with signs, babies

need to learn (and quickly do) that the sign stands for many different yet similar things. If you use the sign *dog* whenever you and your baby encounter any type of dog, he will learn that the sign stands for all dogs—real dogs, toy dogs, pictures of dogs—not just the family pet. Use the *more* sign to ask your baby if he wants more cereal or more juice, or if he would like to read a book over again. Use the *all done* sign when he has finished his milk, when airplanes fly out of sight, and when the bathwater is "all gone" down the drain. (Don't worry; babies quite naturally generalize *all done* to mean "all gone.")

Repeating a sign each time you encounter a different example of the same object or concept teaches your baby that, just as with words, signs can refer to any member of a category. Before long she will begin to figure out exactly what features the members of a category share. In other words, she will have developed a concept of that object. Such concepts, whether they deal with dogs versus cats, hot versus cold, or up versus down, are the building blocks of a baby's intelligence. By focusing a baby's attention on the things in the world around her, the Baby Signs program helps to speed this process along.

8. Be Flexible and Accept Your Baby's Signing Attempts

Even if you have chosen to teach your baby all ASL signs, it's important to be flexible and accepting of even the most basic attempts on your baby's part to use a sign. Just as with first words, babies' first signs quite often only approximate the adult versions, especially when a sign is complex. This is especially true for ASL signs that require two movements (such as *brother* and *sister*) or even finger spelling *and* a movement (such as *bubbles* and *fan*). Young babies, if they try at all, are most likely to attempt only one part of the sign. Always enthusiastically acknowledge his attempts to communicate with you and continue to use the correct form. He will follow your lead as soon as he develops the ability to put the two parts together.

Flexibility also leaves room for baby-created signs. Once your baby realizes that you pay attention to his signs, he may find opportunities to create some on his own. In fact, all babies try to use signs to communicate, even those whose parents have never heard of signing with hearing babies. The problem is that most parents are so focused on speech that they never even notice. The result is frustration on both sides. In contrast, you'll be on the lookout for baby creations.

9. Be Patient

The younger your baby is when you begin signing, the longer it will take her to start using signs herself. In addition, as we discuss below, all children learn at their own pace. (See "Differences Among Babies" on page 46). It can often take a month or longer before your baby starts using signs. The rewards of having this rich way of communicating are well worth the wait.

In children's development, whether walking or talking, everything takes time. Children must practice over and over again before they learn, and then master, a new skill. Just because your baby is not yet using signs does not mean she is not taking it all in. Children learn to talk at all different rates. Learning to sign is no different. Some children do not learn to talk until after most of their peers, and then they start speaking in full sentences. Just as you would not give up on teaching a late talker how to speak, don't give up on teaching a late signer to sign. She may just be too busy working on another task—like walking!

10. Remember, Make Learning Fun

Make sure you give your child lots of recognition and encouragement when teaching signs, and make the learning a natural part of everyday life. And when he tries a sign—like *flower*—a broad smile and an enthusiastic "You're right! That is a flower" go a long way toward making learning fun for him. Children are also surprisingly sensitive to subtle messages of displeasure or disappointment and sometimes become hesitant to try again. So, be sure to notice and reward early efforts, and your baby will soon be using signs to join you in your conversations. Remember, the more enthusiastic you are about signing, the more enthusiastic your baby will be.

Your Baby's Progress

As with the excitement that comes at a baby's first word, parents rejoice at their baby's first sign. Seeing your baby use a sign is an easily observable indicator that she is on her way to "talking" before she can talk. But what about days, weeks, or even months when you are enthusiastically signing without any apparent progress on the part of your baby? Just because your baby is not yet using signs herself does not mean she is not making progress. In fact, there may be a lot going on in that little head of hers, piecing together all the bits of information in anticipation of producing her first sign. There are a number of ways you can tell that your baby is catching on to this new language.

Watching Your Hands

One of the first things you may notice is that your baby begins to pay more attention to your hands. He will find your signing quite intriguing and will begin to watch you in anticipation of a new "word." You may even find that he will bring a toy or book to you, then look at your hands as if asking for a sign. These behaviors show he is beginning to understand that these signs are important for connecting with you. As an indication of early progress, watch how your baby watches you.

Understanding Signs

Watch for evidence that your baby understands the meaning of your signs. Just as babies understand more words than they can say, they also comprehend signs before they use them. For example, if your baby looks toward the dog when you use the *dog* sign or brings you the toy fish from the bathtub when you sign *fish*, these behaviors show that she understands what the signs mean.

Imitating Signs

Of course, the most important evidence of progress is your baby's first attempts to imitate you immediately after you use a sign. The excitement parents feel when their babies begin to use signs to "talk" about things is indescribable. Watch for any effort your baby makes to imitate a sign, no matter how awkward these first attempts might be, and respond enthusiastically. Keep in mind that babies' first words often sound quite different from adult words. For example, even though an adult says "ball," a baby is likely to say "ba." Babies try their best, but it's not easy to master the complexities of clearly articulating the sounds of language. Despite the crudeness of these attempts, parents still provide lots of acknowledgement and encouragement. If a baby says, "goggie" or "nana," parents enthusiastically respond, "That's right, that's a doggie!" or "Oh, you want a banana?" The same happens as your baby is learning signs.

Signing When Asked

When no longer reliant on seeing you sign in order to produce a sign herself, your baby will begin to answer with a sign when you ask her a question such as "What's that?" or "Which book do you want to read?" Although not yet initiating signs herself, using signs to respond to questions is a giant step up on the ladder of progress. Going through picture books and asking "What's that?" is a great way to prompt your baby to practice signing and to strengthen the connection between the sign, the object, and the word, especially when your baby signs *flower* and you reply "That's right! That's a flower."

Signing Spontaneously

Just as parents eagerly await their baby's first word, signing families await their baby's first spontaneous use of signs, the hallmark of true signing communication. It is easy to understand the excitement parents feel the first time their baby reaches out to make a connection from his mind to theirs. It's also undeniable evidence of how smart their baby really is!

Differences Among Babies

Every parent wants to know how long it takes a baby to show the progress just described. Days? Weeks? Months? We have seen cases where each one of these

Every Baby's Timeline Is Different

Q: *Why has my sister's eleven-month-old daughter already learned six signs and four words, whereas my fourteen-month-old son doesn't seem interested in either? What does this mean about my baby's development?*

A: Nothing—except that your son's priorities may be different. Remember, babies have their own interests, motivations, and timetables. Some babies begin to use both signs and words during their first year and continue to develop lots of each at about the same rate. Others learn signs early and rely on them heavily until they develop words months later. Still other babies develop only a few signs but let go quickly even of these because they are learning new words so fast that they don't need the help of their signs for very long. Finally, some babies, especially those more interested in motor challenges, take longer learning both signs and words and rely on both until late in their second year to meet their communication needs. The bottom-line lesson we have learned from all these children is that what is important is to be patient and appreciate your baby's specific preferences and developmental priorities.

was true—and for very good reasons. As we discussed in the section "When to Start Signing" (page 31), the speed with which a baby catches on will depend on lots of things: her age, the number of times she sees the sign, whether she's "into" signs already, her interest in the object being named, and even whether she'd rather be doing something other than communicating at that moment—like reading books or simply climbing the bookshelves. The important thing to remember is to make signing such a natural part of your conversations with her that the signs will be there when she needs them to be.

Expect Your Baby's Age to Make a Difference

Your baby's age when you begin using the Baby Signs program is clearly a factor in determining how long it will take your baby to catch on. Generally speaking, the younger your baby, the longer it will take him to learn his first signs. To understand this, think back to the first time you held out a rattle for your baby to grasp. If he was very young—say, two or three months old—his eyes crossed as he tried to focus on it, his hands flailed out in front of him, and his legs kicked for no good reason at all. Meanwhile the rattle stayed put with you. But if, instead, he was five or six months old when the rattle first came along, he probably fumbled a bit and then quickly mastered the grasping motion.

Few parents are surprised that it takes time for very young babies to learn a complicated business like grasping objects. After all, lots of skills come together in this one act. The same is true for learning signs. The younger the baby, the harder it is to pull together the memory, motor, and attention skills necessary to learn those first few signs. That's why older babies often catch on to signing more quickly than younger babies. But no matter what age your baby is when she achieves this first-sign milestone, once the first few signs are learned, she will clearly be on her way.

Given that your baby is likely to learn more quickly if you begin later, you might be thinking, "Why not just wait?" One reason not to wait is simply that it would be a shame to waste the many opportunities to communicate with your baby that the Baby Signs program would allow in those intervening months.

But something else would be lost, too. Remember, our research shows that the Baby Signs experience actually helps your baby learn how to talk. The sooner your child starts signing, the sooner these positive effects will become evident. That's why it pays to begin helping your baby learn signs as soon as you see evidence that your baby is ready. (See the "When to Start Teaching Signs" box on page 33.)

Remember That Each Baby Is Unique

Besides age, your baby's unique temperament and personality will make a big difference in how quickly she learns to sign. We are repeating this point because parents are often so concerned about the speed of their own child's development relative to other children that they miss the magic of the unfolding of their child's unique timeline of accomplishment.

Babies are also unique in terms of setting their own priorities, too. For some babies, communication is a top concern, and anything, including signs, that enables them to connect with other people is placed high on their to-do list. For other babies, motor milestones are more intriguing and take center stage. We can't tell you how many parents have told us that their baby seemed uninterested—or temporarily lost interest—in signing until he conquered the challenge of learning to walk or climb. This was certainly true of Linda's son, Kai, who didn't begin signing until his first birthday—two weeks after he was finally able to toddle around on his own. After that, it was off to the races in both domains!

Sometimes it is impossible to pinpoint exactly why babies respond to signing at a different pace. All we can say is that they just do. Consider, for example, the experiences of Samantha and Robin. Both little girls were twelve months old when their parents began using the Baby Signs program. Extremely energetic, Samantha was already showing an interest in sharing things with those around her, a good indication of readiness. Sure enough, Samantha caught on within two weeks, surprising her mother by signing *more* at mealtime to ask for more cheese. From that point, there was no stopping her. Over the next two months she added more than twenty other signs and quite a few words. Given such an impressive "vocabulary," Samantha was one of the most articulate fourteen-month-old children we had ever met!

Robin's experience was different but equally successful. At twelve months, Robin was a cheerful little girl, content to play with toys but also ready to greet almost anyone with a broad smile and uplifted arms. Robin's mom began modeling signs at this point and was unusually enthusiastic and creative in finding opportunities to use them. But unlike Samantha, Robin took two months rather than two weeks before she produced her first sign. The occasion was at Thanksgiving dinner, and the motivation was the flower centerpiece on the table. As the family members gathered around the table and Robin was put into her booster seat, she spied the colorful flower arrangement. Without a moment's hesitation, she looked to her mom, wrinkled up her nose, and "sniffed" away, showing her mastery of the baby-friendly sign for *flower*. Robin proceeded to add fifteen other signs to her repertoire in the space of three weeks. And she didn't stop there. She eventually added an additional thirty-five signs before words burst forth in a gush at eighteen months. Robin's mother had clearly been rewarded for her patience.

There's simply no way to know why these two babies started to sign at different times. Many factors play a role in the pace at which babies begin to use signs. Our best advice is to watch for the behaviors described earlier that indicate readiness, introduce the starter signs we highlight in Chapter 4, and use them patiently and consistently. In doing so, you will be providing your baby interesting food for thought no matter how long it takes him to produce signs himself.

> Babies love using their signs when looking at books to "say" what they see on each page.

Enrich Your Baby's Signing Experience

You can do several things to enhance learning and make signing easy and fun for your baby. Other signing families have told us that looking through picture books together, singing songs and playing games that include signs, watching signing DVDs, and incorporating the whole family into the signing endeavor are among the best ways to bring the Baby Signs program into your lives in a relaxed and enjoyable way. Here we look more closely at each of these suggestions.

Take Advantage of Books

Reading picture books provides a range of opportunities to use signs. Babies love to flip through picture books and have their parents tell them what is on each page. You'll quickly discover that books provide a rich source of new signing ideas. ABC books, for example, typically have pictures of common objects for each letter, many of which can have sign "names," too: A for *apple* or *airplane*,

B for *butterfly* or *bunny*, C for *cat* or *cow*, and so on. We're not suggesting that you need to use a sign for every object, just that you be open to the opportunity books present to introduce signs you may not have tried yet. (The Baby Signs dictionary at the back of the book is full of good ideas.)

In addition, Baby Signs board books like *Baby Signs: Time to Eat* and *Baby Signs: Favorites* are specifically designed to help you introduce signing in a fun way. (Visit www.babysigns.com for many signing book options.) Simple story books, like Margaret Wise Brown's *Goodnight Moon*, with all its pictures of the *moon* and the *mouse*, or Dr. Seuss's *Cat in the Hat*, with all its *cats* and *hats*, are fun to enhance with signs. Babies love reading them over and over, which makes it easy to work in lots of practice with the signs your baby is learn-

ing. Watch for specific things that your baby likes as you turn the pages. Try out some signs, and delight in the opportunity the Baby Signs program gives you to generate a two-way interaction. The more your baby sees you using signs with his favorite books, the sooner he will learn that he too can "talk" about the dog or cat or bird on the page. Fun and engaging experi- ences such as these early in life go a long way toward developing a lifelong love of reading.

Use Songs, Rhymes, and Games

In addition, songs, nursery rhymes, and fingerplay games are fun ways to teach signs. Try teaching your baby the *spider* sign while singing "Eensy-Weensy Spider." This is an example of when you might choose to use a baby-friendly sign instead of the ASL sign. Since rubbing index fingertips together to rep- resent the spider going up the water spout commonly accompanies the song, it might be less confusing to your baby to have only one sign for *spider*. You can always shift to the ASL sign later if your goal is to continue signing with your child beyond her preverbal years. Use this *spider* sign to label lots of spiders—real ones, rubber ones, and pictures. The goal is simply to provide your baby with lots of opportunities to learn that rubbing two index fingers together means "spider" and can work just as well as the word until she learns to say it.

It's also fun—and helpful—to make up little poems and games to introduce signs. Here's one we've shared with lots of parents over the years:

Butterfly, butterfly tickles your nose
Butterfly, butterfly tickles your toes
Butterfly, butterfly flies around
Butterfly, butterfly lands on the ground.

Using a *butterfly* sign, flutter your fingers gently on your baby's nose and then on his toes, fly your *butterfly* hands from side to side, and finally bring them to rest on the ground.

Songs, rhymes, and games such as these are enjoyable and easily repeated. Most of all, they make learning fun. Once you become aware of how easy it is to teach signs with songs and rhymes, you will begin to see lots of opportunities.

Consider Signing DVDs Produced Just for Babies

One of the easiest and most enjoyable ways to teach your baby important signs is by watching DVDs specifically designed to help babies learn signs. But are DVDs good for babies?

Perhaps you've heard the concern voiced by pediatricians that babies under age two should watch no television at all. This strong prohibition was issued by the American Academy of Pediatrics a decade ago as a safeguard against parents who expose their children to hours and hours of general, noneducational programming, using the TV simply as a babysitter that keeps them occupied and happy without providing any lasting benefits.

Since that time, more and more research studies have revealed that the *content* of what's watched matters a great deal. In fact, educational programming specifically designed for very young children can have positive effects on their development. For example, watching television shows that elicit participation, like *Dora the Explorer* and *Blue's Clues*, actually facilitates language development, as do shows that feature simple language in ways children can follow, like *Clifford the Big Red Dog*.

It's also critical that programs for babies avoid the frantic pacing and complex imagery typical of shows for older children and adults. In fact, new research has shown that even having adult fare playing in the background tends to disrupt infant play behavior. Our many years of research with very young children have taught us that in order for infant minds to concentrate well enough to absorb information, pacing must be *very* slow, images must be visually simple, and important points must be repeated over and over and over. All of this may not make exciting fare for Mom and Dad, but the result, especially when DVDs are designed to actually teach babies something useful (like signs), is programming that is demonstrably good for babies. (Visit www.babysigns.com for DVD suggestions.)

Of course, we want to stress that the very best way to help your baby learn from the DVDs is to join her, modeling the signs yourself right along with the characters. Doing so not only maximizes learning, but also provides the one-on-one attention that is critical to keeping your relationship strong and positive.

Make Signing a Family Affair

The Baby Signs program enriches family interactions, so encourage others to get involved. Older brothers and sisters love to help teach the baby new signs, and sitting down to read their baby sister or brother a book is more fun with signs. The parents in one family had their six-year-old daughter draw and color lots of pictures of the things her baby brother was learning signs for—flowers, monkeys, fish, turtles, and birds. Her creations were then posted on the refrigerator, taped to doors and windows, and even pinned to her sweatshirt. She took great pleasure in pointing to the pictures and showing her brother the signs. And you can imagine the pride she felt when he began to use the signs himself. Given the difficulty many parents have in helping older children accept a new baby, the opportunity the Baby Signs program provides for brothers and sisters to join the team is definitely a plus.

Grandparents also enjoy being included as a part of the team and love showing off their smart grandchild who can "talk" before she can talk. Once they know that signs actually make learning to talk easier, they become enthusiastic. And it's no secret that grandparents take particular joy in playing games and teaching songs, both wonderful sources of signs. Riding horsie on Grandpa's knee or singing "Little Bunny Foo Foo" with Grandma are among many a child's fondest memories, and being able to request these games using signs lends added pleasure.

Keeping Your Eye on the Right Prize

Now that you are ready to start teaching your baby to use signs, it's time for an important reminder. Success with the Baby Signs program is not about how many signs your baby learns. It's about how the signs he learns—no matter how many or how few—make daily life easier and more satisfying. Although some children in our National Institutes of Health study learned more than forty signs, a significant number learned a dozen or fewer. The reasons for these differences are many. Some children are just more interested than others, some families start later than others, and some family circumstances are more conducive to teaching signs than others (for example, having older siblings or childcare teachers to help). Yet even the families where relatively few signs were used reported that frustration had been reduced and positive communication increased. So, as you move on to Chapter 4, in which we introduce a wide range of signs, remember that you don't have to teach your baby every one of them. Our goal is simply to give you a selection from which to pick based on your knowledge of your own baby's interests and needs.

CHAPTER 4

Signs, Signs, and More Signs

To tell the truth, when my wife started teaching our son signs, I thought it was a bit silly. But I began to see that the whole sign language idea made a lot of sense when Adam began using the more *sign after just a week. A few days later he started signing* eat *and* drink *and stopped whining so much at the dinner table every night. So I joined forces with my wife and began showing Adam lots of signs. It was amazing how quickly our son caught on. What a world of difference those simple signs have made to our lives!*

—Skeptical father of nineteen-month-old Adam

WITH A WHOLE WORLD OF SIGNS FROM WHICH TO CHOOSE, getting started can seem overwhelming. But don't worry. Our purpose with this chapter is to ease you into signing with your child so that you feel excitement from the very start. And we're in a good position to do so given that, since we first began our research on the Baby Signs program in the 1980s, we have helped countless families get started on the road to signing success.

Based on these experiences, we have learned that certain signs are particularly good to start with, both because they are easy for babies to do and because they represent especially useful concepts. We have also learned that choosing signs that relate to the routines of daily life is the best way to make sure your baby sees the signs regularly and gets the repetition necessary for learning.

But focusing on routines is important for another reason. Research shows that babies both need and enjoy routines in their daily lives. To fully appreciate the comfort that routines provide everyone, children included, think back to the last time you started a new job. In addition to dealing with unfamiliar people and tasks, chances are you didn't know what kinds of events to expect each day or the order in which to expect them. As the days passed, things gradually fell into a comfortable routine, and both your mind and your emotions were free to focus on something more productive than simply trying to predict "What's next!?"

The lesson here is that, like adults, children thrive when there is predictability to their days. They are happier and healthier, learn more about their world, and are a lot easier to get along with. Something else good is happening too. Children not only take comfort in routines but also take great pride in having mastered a routine so well that they can announce the order of events to us.

That's why the signs we are suggesting in this chapter are divided into categories representing such routines—like mealtime, bathtime, and bedtime. In fact, daily routines are so helpful to babies that we have used these same routines as the basis for five of our six Baby Signs DVDs designed specifically to help babies learn signs in a fun and easy way.

Each of the following five sections is devoted to a different daily routine. Our focus in a sixth section is on pets. Although not representative of a specific routine, there's no denying that pets play a major role in the daily lives of many families and are, therefore, meaningful to children.

We begin each section by briefly explaining the relevance of that routine or category to the lives of babies and by presenting in some detail two signs that we know from experience to be great starter signs. If your baby is already saying the word for one of these concepts, then there is obviously no need to learn the sign. Instead, choose a substitute that will add something new to the list of things your baby can talk about in regard to that routine. For example, if your baby is already saying *milk*, which is fairly easy for some babies to say, then choose another sign pertinent to mealtime to begin working on. To help you in choosing appropriate substitutes, we list many additional signs, both in this chapter and in the Baby Signs dictionary at the back of the book.

Once your baby has caught on to signing and is watching, understanding, or using at least some of these easy starter signs, she is ready to use signs for things as divergent as *monkeys* and *medicine* and *telephones* and *tigers*. As with any aspect of learning, however, it is better to crawl before you walk. Start off slowly, be sensitive to your baby's pace, and you both will be off and running before you know it!

Mealtime

Over and over we hear from parents that signs pertaining to eating and drinking are the first ones they see their babies use—sometimes as early as six months of age if parents have been using the signs consistently for a while. Although parents are often surprised by this, we never are. Research has shown that babies, from the day they are born, are more likely to learn things that relate in some way to food and feeding than they are to learn anything else. The reason is pretty simple: because food is critical to survival, anything that can help ensure that food is on its way when hunger strikes is going to be an especially valuable tool.

Of course, the very first tool that babies use to signal hunger is crying. Although crying eventually works to get them fed, the fact that young babies also need to use crying to indicate other feeling states (like being sleepy, cold, or sick) makes it less efficient than a hunger-specific message. And that's exactly why babies are eager to substitute simple signs like *milk* and *eat* at such young ages—and is also why

> Because food is so critical to survival, babies are especially primed to learn things associated with eating—including mealtime signs like *milk* and *eat*.

Milk   *Eat*

we are focusing on these two signs as excellent mealtime starter signs.

As babies near their first birthday, however, both their minds and their palates have progressed to the point that even more specific mealtime signs are needed. Not only do they know in general that they are hungry, they also know more specifically whether they are ready for their *bib*, would like something to *drink* or would rather have *cereal* to *eat*, want *more* of what they already have or, instead, are ready to get *down* from their chair because they are *all done*. Signs like these help ensure that mealtimes are happy times rather than occasions for tantrums and tears. And they work for snacktime, too. Are Goldfish crackers a mainstay of your baby's diet? Use the *cracker* sign, or even try the *fish* sign. We can't tell you how many times we've seen babies calmly asking for Goldfish crackers by using the *more* and *fish* signs together. And when there are no more left to give, the *all done* sign can convey the bad news.

In addition to these signs, the Baby Signs dictionary also includes other signs for specific foods: *apple*, *banana*, *bread*, *carrot*, *cheese*, *chicken*, *cookie*, *cracker*, *egg*, *fruit*, *grapes*, *hot dog*, *juice*, *orange*, *peas*, and *yogurt*. Our research has also shown a number of nonfood signs to be especially relevant to mealtime: the *hot* sign can be useful to let parents know when food is too

The Baby Signs Program in Action

More than Crackers "All Gone"

Still chewing his first cracker, fourteen-month-old Austin toddled over to his mom and signed *cracker* followed by the *all done* sign. "Oh, you want another cracker," said his mom as she gave him one. A few minutes later Austin was back again. Instead of requesting a third cracker, however, Austin signed *spider*. Looking down, his mom saw a spider on a collision course with her foot. She was just about to say, "That's right, that is a spider," when Austin smashed it with his shoe, grinned up at her, and signed *all done*. There was no doubt about it—the spider, like the cracker, was indeed "all done!"

hot; the *want* and *down* signs help babies express desires, and the *please* and *thank you* signs enable children to learn rules of politeness at young ages. And, finally, in line with our commitment to helping babies talk about the things that are really on their minds, we've also included in the Baby Signs dictionary two all-time baby favorites—*candy* and *ice cream*!

Bathtime

"Splish-splash, I was taking a bath…!" If babies could talk, we're sure the lyrics to this classic song would be on their hit parade. Why? Because most babies truly enjoy bathtime and the predictable features that make up their own personal bathtime routine. Whether they are splashing solo (Mom or Dad close by their side, of course) or with an older brother or sister to share the fun, the opportunity to be unencumbered by clothes and free to play is a highlight of daily life for most children.

Research shows, however, that there's more to bathtime than pure play. Beyond the splishing and the splashing, there's a whole lot of learning going on. That's right. While it may look like pure fun when little Madeleine pushes her yellow duckie and her rubber frog under the water only to see them pop up again, the truth is that Madeleine is also watching carefully to see whether both toys pop up the same way, or one pops up faster or slower or even upside down.

And then there's the magic of the washcloth—first floating on the top of the water, then gradually becoming heavier and heavier as water is absorbed and it starts to sink. These are all little scientific experiments that add incrementally

Bath   *Bubbles*

to a baby's knowledge of how the world works.

The two bathtime signs we suggest as good starter signs are *bath* and *bubbles*. The *bath* sign relates in obvious ways to the bathtime routine and is especially easy to do. The *bubble* sign is a particular favorite—as is the inevitable combination *more* and *bubbles*. Babies simply adore bubbles, which is why more than one parent has wooed her child into the bathtub with bubble solution and a wand.

And what's bathtime without water and toys like rubber ducks and frogs to play with? Because they are easy to do, the *water*, *duck*, and *frog* signs also make good starter signs, as does the *toothbrush* sign, another important part of the bathtime routine.

Other signs relevant to the bath routine that you'll find in the Baby Signs dictionary include *boat*, *cold*, *dirty*, *fish*, *hair*, *hot*, *hurt*, *shampoo*, *soap*, and *wash*. After all, *water* can be too *hot*, too *cold*, or *all done* (*all gone*) down the drain; washing *hair* is part of the routine; *shampoo* and *soap* can get in the eyes and *hurt*; *fish* and *boats* can be as much fun in the tub as *ducks* and *frogs*, and everyone knows the whole purpose of the bath is to *wash* so you're no longer *dirty*!

The Baby Signs Program in Action

When It's Too Hot to Trot

Twelve-month-old Keegan routinely used the baby-friendly sign for **hot** (a blowing motion) when his food or even bathwater was too hot. A novel use, however, occurred one day at the swimming pool. As his mother headed toward the water with Keegan toddling at her side, he suddenly stopped and began blowing furiously. Quickly recognizing the sign, she figured out the problem, and swept him up into her arms. What was it? Hot concrete! Had he simply started crying when his feet began to burn, precious time would surely have been lost. In fact, his mother might even have interpreted his crying as stubbornness and pulled him along even harder!

Bedtime

As we've said before, children love and need routines in their lives, and the bedtime routine is an extremely important example. Pull any "how to get your baby to sleep" book at random off the bookstore shelf and you'll find the bedtime routine touted as critical to success. Why? There are a number of reasons why establishing a stable bedtime routine helps children make the transition to sleep.

1. The traditional bedtime routine calls for reducing noise, activity, and even lighting in order to help the child wind down, thereby making it more likely that she will relax enough to fall asleep easily.

2. The consistency of the routine night after night creates a feeling of inevitability in the child's mind, that there's no use protesting. In fact, just as sitting in one's favorite easy chair becomes a trigger to send an adult off to sleep in front of the TV, so can the steps of the bedtime routine start to automatically make a child's eyelids get heavier and heavier.

3. Children love figuring out what comes next in a sequence of events. Doing so makes them feel smart and less anxious. In terms of the bedtime routine, the fact that even very young children take pride in figuring out the steps means that they are likely to cooperate or "buy into" the routine.

It's worth pointing out that adding signs to the bedtime routine is a great way to make it even more likely that your child will feel positive about bedtime because the signs provide the child with a way to take an active role. "Book? You're right. We always read a book together before we turn out the light."

With signs for bedtime words at her fingertips, your child will have a way to show you that she knows the rules of the game. What's more, she'll not only be able to remind you that it's storytime, but she'll also be able to tell you which book she wants to read, the one about the *dog* or the one about the *bunny* or that old favorite about saying goodnight to the *moon*. Of course, you also have to be prepared for the inevitable sign-plus-sign combination *more* and *book*, no matter how many books you've already read. (Hint: That's when you use the sign for *all done!*)

So, what are some good bedtime starter signs? The two we've chosen to highlight are *book*, which we've just discussed, and *sleep/bed*. There are several reasons why *sleep/bed* is an especially good choice. First, it's easy for everyone to remember and interpret. Second, babies often use the sign to let their parents know when they are tired and want to go to sleep! Being able to signal this important message helps prevent the kinds of meltdowns and overtiredness that often end up making it harder to get children to sleep.

Two other good bedtime starter signs are *moon* and *star*, signs that can help your baby talk about pictures in popular bedtime books as well as what he sees out the window. And, of course, there are the *light* and *love* signs—because, at the end of the bedtime routine, it's *lights* out and one last hug full of *love*.

Many other signs relevant to the bedtime routine are included in the Baby Signs dictionary. For example, some children want to hear a lullaby at bedtime and can use the *song* sign to ask for it. Others may use the *pacifier* or the *potty* sign to

> **The Baby Signs Program in Action**
>
> **Stars in Her Eyes**
> Fourteen-month-old Abby was visiting her aunt. When bedtime rolled around, her dad tucked her into bed in her cousin's room. Just after he switched off the light and closed the door, he heard Abby calling "Dada!" in an excited voice. Switching the light back on and peeking in, he saw Abby wiggling her fingers in the air—her **star** sign. "Stars?" he said, looking around. "I'm afraid I don't see any, sweetheart." He settled her down and once more headed to the door. Glancing into the room one last time as he switched off the lights, he suddenly realized what Abby had seen. The ceiling was covered with fluorescent stars! Invisible with the lights on, the stars appeared as if by magic as soon as they were off. "You're right! There are stars!" said Jim as he lifted her up to touch them. Without signs, Jim knew, this lovely moment wouldn't have happened.

make equally important requests. In addition to signs for these things, the dictionary includes the following signs that might be useful at bedtime: *afraid*, *bear* (for teddy bear), *blanket*, *clean up*, *cold*, *Daddy*, *diaper*, *drink*, *hot*, *milk*, *Mommy*, *pajamas*, and

Book   Sleep/Bed

want. And, finally, we're all familiar with the all-time bedtime favorite—one last *drink* of *water*.

Getting Dressed

The routine of getting dressed, as well as the even more popular getting undressed, is intriguing to babies and toddlers. But why the attraction? In part, their fascination is due to the very fact that getting dressed is a routine—that is, that there's a very predictable sequence of events that occurs so frequently that it is easy for babies to learn. A diaper always comes first, followed by shirt and pants, followed by socks and shoes. Second, each object involved in the routine has not only a particular place in the sequence, but also a particular place on the

body: hats go on the top of one's head, diapers go on one's bottom, and socks and shoes go on one's feet. In fact, some of the earliest humor we see babies react to and even display themselves has to do with violations of the getting-dressed routine: Dad putting a diaper on his head or letting socks dangle from his ears is worthy of the Comedy Channel in a baby's eyes!

As babies begin to fine-tune their motor skills, however, getting dressed takes on a whole new mystique. It becomes a set of physical challenges to be mastered as a badge of honor attesting to one's blossoming independence. The good news is that such independence, when finally achieved, frees parents from having to do everything for the baby. The bad news is that, in the meantime, life can be a series of challenges for parents too. It's the rare parent who doesn't know the desperate feeling of being in a hurry to get out the door only to find herself stopped in her tracks by a toddler struggling determinedly to put his shoes on himself. Since at least 50 percent of the time he's trying to put the right shoe on the left foot and the left shoe on the right foot, Mom is in trouble! In fact, the high-pitched wail "I do it!" is often first uttered in regard to parts of the getting-dressed routine.

The Baby Signs Program in Action

A Hair-Raising Experience
When a man with dreadlocks sat down across from fourteen-month-old Sam and his mother on the bus, Sam turned to her and signed *hat*. "Oh, honey, I know it looks like a hat, but it's really hair," whispered his mother. Sam turned back to the man, stared intently, and very emphatically repeated the *hat* sign. Catching on to the situation, the young man invited Sam to feel his dreadlocks for himself. No sooner had Sam's fingers touched the man's hair than Sam, his eyes wide with surprise, made the *hair* sign. The message was as clear as if he had spoken the words: "It *is* hair!"

From all the signs relevant to this important part of daily life, we've chosen *diaper* and *hat* to highlight as good starter signs. The choice of *diaper* is pretty obvious. Although we firmly believe, based on a thorough review of research on the topic, that it is best for babies, parents, and the environment to complete potty training by age two, diapers are clearly still relevant during the time babies are

Diaper   *Hat*

most likely to be signing. The beauty of the *diaper* sign is that babies can use it to let others know when they need a change, thereby making life easier for adults attending to more than one child at a time.

Hats, in contrast, are less frequently a part of the getting-dressed routine. But that fact in no way diminishes babies' fascination with them. Babies love hats and see them everywhere! There are baseball hats, winter hats, and firefighter hats, just to name a few. Read a book with a baby who knows the *hat* sign and you'll be amazed at the number of characters wearing hats. Take a stroll to the park and you'll find yourself talking about motorcycle helmets when she notices the motorcycle rider stopped at the traffic light. Adding to the fun is the fact that the *hat* sign is one of the very easiest signs to learn; there's certainly nothing complicated about patting one's head.

> Babies are delighted when they can share with others what they see and hear using signs. Parents who teach signs only for obvious needs, like *milk*, *eat*, and *more*, miss out on this precious window into their child's world.

Other good starter signs that pertain to getting dressed include *socks*, *shoes*, and *comb*. With feet safely tucked into the first two and hair neatly arranged with the help of the third, all that's left before going out the door is something for which there's another good starter sign: *coat*. Additional signs relevant to getting dressed are available in the Baby Signs dictionary. These include *clothes*, *gentle*, *hair*, *help*, *hot*, *hurt*, and *where*.

At the Park

New parents often comment that they are amazed by what their children notice. "She finds even the littlest things so fascinating that I'm seeing the world with new eyes too!" It's true. As adults we've become so familiar with the world around us that we tend not to see even things right before our eyes. Babies, on the other hand, don't miss anything. Their faces light up when a raindrop hits a puddle, when snowflakes melt on their tongues, when a caterpillar crawls on their finger, and even when their shadow follows them down the street. The world is a magical place to young children, full of things to see, hear, and, most important of all, to share with the people they love.

And where do many of these memorable experiences occur? At the park! Whether it's the vast acres of Central Park in New York City or a tiny plot of land tucked in among tightly packed houses, the park tends to hold a privileged place in the lives of many children. Now, with signs at her fingertips, your baby will be able to share her discoveries with you. No longer will her desire to call your attention to what she finds so exciting be limited to just pointing in a general direction. With signs she can tell you whether it's a *bird*, *squirrel*, *butterfly*, or *airplane* that has captured her attention.

In fact, we believe that one reason signing spurs both verbal language and intellectual development (as reflected in the higher IQs we found in our research) is that signs enable babies to draw their parents' attention to the specific things that are particularly interesting to *them*—which may be very different from what their parents are thinking about. The typical parental response, in turn, is to join in conversation with the baby by talking about that item, filling in details while the baby listens very attentively because, after all, *he* chose the topic!

> Baby: [Signs *butterfly*.]
> Mom: "You're right! There's a butterfly! It's a blue butterfly—like the one in your book. Remember? It grew out of a caterpillar."

Tidbit by tidbit, a baby's knowledge of the world grows, and signing gets the process started earlier than would otherwise be the case if babies had to wait for words to communicate.

The two signs relevant to the park that we've chosen to highlight as good starter signs are *flower* and *ball*. Both of these ASL signs are especially easy to do and represent items that are particularly meaningful to babies. In addition to real flowers in the park, there are flowers in books, magazines, and paintings, as well as on wallpaper, clothes, and greeting cards. There are also many things that aren't flowers but look like them—like broccoli and geometric designs. In fact, flowers are so salient to babies that the baby-friendly version (sniffing) is among the signs babies are most likely to create on their own.

Flower　　　　*Ball*

The *ball* sign, standing as it does for one of the most consistently popular childhood toys of any era, is also a good choice. And, as is true of the *flower* sign, the *ball* sign is frequently used to label things that aren't balls but look like them—like oranges, globe lights, and even the moon!

Moreover, what's a trip to the park without a stop at the slide and the swings— and a way for babies to ask to have another turn on each (*more* and *slide*, and *more* and *swing*)? These are signs babies really appreciate, as are the *butterfly* and *tree* signs, not only because they are common at the park, but also because there are lots of pictures of them for babies to label in favorite books.

Many other signs relevant to the park are included in the Baby Signs dictionary. For example, there are *airplanes* overhead, *boats* and *ducks* on the lake, *squirrels* running up and down *trees*, *dogs* catching Frisbees, *clouds* in the sky, *bikes* passing by, and, best of all, other *girls*, *boys*, and even *babies* to *play* with. In addition to signs for these items, the dictionary includes the following signs that might be useful in outings with your baby: *bird, bug, car, coat, cold, fish, frog, go, home, hot, noise, play, rain, snow, spider, sun, swim,* and *walk*.

Animals and Pets

Animals in general hold a special spot in the hearts of children. In fact, more than a third of the average baby's earliest words are names for animals, with *cat, dog, duck,* and *bunny* leading the pack. And because our research shows that the same is true for signs, we focus on some of the easiest and most popular ones here.

But first, have you ever wondered why it is that children find animals so fascinating? Although they probably never knew the scientific answer to that question, poets and storytellers across the ages have sensed the attraction and used it to both entertain and teach. Mary and her faithful little lamb, Little Bo Peep and her poor lost sheep, and Old Mother Hubbard and her poor hungry dog are just a few of many examples. And whom do we traditionally thank for these rhymes? None other than one more famous animal, Mother Goose!

You may already have sensed your child's fascination with dogs and cats, bunnies and birds. What lies behind it is really quite simple, researchers tell us. As young babies begin looking around their world, they are automatically attracted to things that move, are brightly colored, and are easy to see. They are fascinated by things that make interesting noises, are capable of interacting with them, and are unpredictable in what they do and how they behave. The most obvious items that fit this description are other people. And in fact, from the day they are born, babies are absolutely fascinated by the faces and voices of the people around them. Fortunately, we feel the same way about them!

The Baby Signs Program in Action

A Fond Memory
This story is from our 1983 research files, when we were first discovering that babies create signs all on their own.

Fifteen-month-old Cheyenne's mom was busy talking with us in the living room when Cheyenne noticed the family dog scratching at the back door. Realizing that her mom wasn't paying attention, Cheyenne toddled into the room, tugged at her mother, and made her self-created sign for *dog* (panting), followed immediately by her self-created sign for *outside* (turning her hand like turning a doorknob). "Excuse me," said her mom matter-of-factly, "I have to let the dog out."

We both still remember grinning at each other. We had just witnessed the magic of signing firsthand.

But humans aren't the only things in the world that meet these criteria. Animals do, too. In sharp contrast to even the most exciting mechanical toy, an animal moves itself around, behaves in unpredictable ways, and makes lots of funny noises. What's more, many of the animals children see at close range have the added advantage of providing what researchers call "contact comfort"—or what most people call being soft and cuddly! Even at a distance, babies find animals about as far from boring as things can be without being human.

Dog

Having signs available to talk about animals helps babies share their observations with the important people in their lives, whether those observations involve real animals, animals in books, animals on TV, or even their favorite stuffed animals. However, when it comes to animals, babies are also surprisingly observant about what they *hear*. Many parents have told us that they would

Cat

never have noticed dogs barking, birds chirping, or cats meowing outside if it hadn't been for their baby's ability to tell them with signs. It's another example of how babies can wake us up to the wonders around us that we're sometimes too busy to notice.

Since dogs and cats are the most common household pets, we've chosen to highlight *dog* and *cat* as good starter signs. At first you may be puzzled by our inclusion of the *dog* sign as a good candidate for a starter sign, given that the ASL form we've chosen requires snapping one's fingers. Our decision to suggest *dog* anyway is based on four factors: (1) dogs are so fascinating to children that they are especially eager to learn a sign; (2) babies can approximate snapping fingers closely enough to be understood; (3) other ASL versions involve slapping the leg, an easy action; and (4) the baby-friendly version, panting with the tongue out, is especially popular among young babies. In fact, back in the 1980s when we gathered research data on signs that babies create on their own, we found that panting for *dog* was one of the most popular. The other starter sign we are suggesting here, *cat*, is quite straightforward: tracing the outline of whiskers on the cheek.

Other good starter signs that provide babies with an easy way to talk about well-loved but nonhuman members of the family include *bird, bunny, fish,* and *turtle.* The Baby Signs dictionary includes many other useful animal signs: *bug, butterfly, chicken, cow, duck, elephant, fish, frog, giraffe, goat, horse, lion, monkey, mouse, pig, sheep, spider, squirrel,* and *zebra.* You'll find that these signs make storytimes with books especially fun for your baby because he can take an active role by labeling animals when you point to them or ask "What's that?" Because exposure to books early in life is known to predict good reading skills and larger vocabularies, we believe that this increased enjoyment of books is another way signing contributes to faster language and intellectual development.

To sum it all up, signs for pets and other animals enable children to become active partners in conversations about a topic they absolutely adore—all creatures great and small.

Choosing Signs to Teach

Completing the following sentences about your baby's favorite things is a good way to decide which signs to introduce to your baby as you start expanding his signing vocabulary. For example, if your baby's favorite nursery rhyme is "Hickory Dickory Dock," the *mouse* sign might be a good choice.

My baby's favorite drink is _____ .

My baby's favorite snack is _____ .

My baby's favorite fruit is _____ .

My baby's favorite playtime toy is _____ .

My baby's favorite bedtime toy is _____ .

My baby's favorite bathtime toy is_____ .

My baby's favorite pet is _____ .

My baby's favorite farm animal is _____ .

My baby's favorite zoo animal is _____ .

My baby's favorite book is _____ .

My baby's favorite song is_____ .

My baby's favorite nursery rhyme is _____ .

CHAPTER 5

Off and Running with Signs

It suddenly seemed like a lightbulb went on in her head, and she began picking up one sign after another. And soon we noticed she was even combining them into little sentences. An airplane or something would disappear, and she'd excitedly sign airplane all done. *It was so great!*

—Mother of fifteen-month-old Laney

BABIES, LIKE THE REST OF US, TAKE GREAT JOY IN NEWLY discovered pleasures, whether those pleasures are toys, tastes, or talents. For example, take learning to walk. Somewhere between nine and fifteen months, babies develop the physical ability to balance on their legs and launch themselves on a seemingly drunken path through space. What a trip—both literally and figuratively. There's simply no doubt that babies revel in this newfound skill, seeing potential destinations everywhere, from the delicate crystal vase across the room to the strange dog across the park. And so our formerly bound-to-the-ground sons and daughters are suddenly off and running, while we parents find ourselves for the first time following instead of leading our babies around the world.

Something very similar, and equally enchanting, happens as babies catch on to signing. Just as Laney's mom said in the quote that introduced this chapter, it's as though the lightbulb goes on. Babies seem to suddenly understand how this naming game works and take great pleasure in finding things to talk about. "A-ha! That's what it's all about! I move my fingers across my cheek and Mommy knows I saw a *cat*!" Suddenly, they are true partners in a world of two-way communication and are eager to lead the way. Grown-ups are no longer the only ones talking. Conversations can now start when the baby wants them to.

With each new sign at their disposal, this insight becomes more firmly entrenched. As it does so, babies begin to listen more attentively to the words you say and watch more closely the things you do. They are eager to get up on their conversational "legs" and set off exploring the world. But exactly what kinds of experiences can you expect once your baby is off and running with signs? That's the question we turn to now.

Here, There, and Everywhere

Do you remember how, once you were expecting a baby, you began to see pregnant women everywhere? Or, having finally decided to buy a particular car, you started to notice how many like it are already on the

road? Where did they all come from? The answer, of course, lies in the heightened awareness that your own situation creates. It's as though you have special radar unconsciously scanning the environment for the things that are momentarily of special importance to you.

The same thing happens to your baby when she learns a new sign or new word. With a new label at her command, she suddenly sees examples everywhere— even in places that you don't expect. For example, for fourteen-month-old Eli, the *apple* sign made even a trip to the grocery store a special adventure, what with apples, apple pies, apple juice, and even pictures of apples on greeting cards. His mother, like many of us, had never realized how pervasive apples were in the environment until Eli set about to find them all. In a similar way, fifteen-month-old Trina had a love affair with her *bird* sign. Everyone expects to find birds out the window or at the park—but at church? Sure enough, embedded in the stained-glass windows over the altar were not one but two ornamental doves, peace symbols to the congregation but just plain *birds* to Trina. At least using a sign was a quiet way to talk about them!

Like these parents, you'll find yourself amazed at how vigilant your baby can be. She may be only a baby, but lots of mental activity is happening for her behind the scenes. And each time your baby tells you about something with a sign, she is providing you with a glimpse into all that activity, enabling you to respond appropriately and enthusiastically.

Feelings Discovered

Being able to identify and talk about one's own emotions and feelings is an important step toward learning how to control them. It is also key to developing the ability to feel empathy for others when they are hurting and need help, a skill that research shows makes children popular with their peers.

> **The Baby Signs Program in Action**
>
> **The Mall Is a Jungle These Days**
> Once thirteen-month-old Kai learned the *crocodile* sign he began to see crocodiles everywhere, including at the mall. Contentedly riding in his stroller one day, Kai suddenly squirmed to face his mom and began to sign *crocodile*, his eyes wide with glee. "What? A crocodile in the mall?" asked his mom, not seeing any herself. He was quite insistent, so she let him out of his stroller, whereupon he toddled over to the store window they had just passed. And there, much to his mom's surprise, they saw plenty of crocodiles—tiny ones in the upper corners of the men's shirts hanging in the window! His mother was absolutely amazed! For his part, Kai was thrilled that his mother had quickly understood and joined him in appreciating his fine discovery.

Signing babies are proving that very young children are much more sophisticated about emotions and feelings than anyone had ever suspected. How do we know? Exciting new evidence comes from a research study by Dr. Claire Vallotton based on detailed videotaped observations of infants and teachers interacting at the Center for Child and Family Studies at the University of California, Davis.

> The fact that babies and toddlers can use signs to label their own and others' emotions has shown very young children to be more cognitively sophisticated than scientists had ever suspected.

At the most basic level, once babies are off and running with signs, they branch out to communicate in fairly precise ways what they are feeling. Being able to do so is a big improvement over relying on facial expressions and crying as nonsigning children must. Crying, in particular, is ambiguous. It is clearly a sign of distress and a call for action on the part of adults, but it doesn't make clear what the problem is. Have you accidentally pinched your baby's skin with a tight diaper? Have you forgotten a favorite toy? Is the bathwater too hot or too cold? Does your baby have an earache? Is your baby simply angry because another child has taken a toy away?

With signs from the Baby Signs program, your baby is much more likely to be able to tell you what the problem is. Among the signs for feelings included in the Baby Signs dictionary are many of the signs Dr. Vallotton observed children use in her study, signs that describe common reasons nine- to thirty-month-old children cry. They include feeling *afraid*, *sad*, *hurt*, and *angry*. Other signs that are useful for communicating feelings include *cold*, *hot*, *stop*, and *gentle*. And then there are signs for specific needs, such as *drink*, *eat*, *pacifier*, and *diaper*. Once you know why your baby is crying, changing those tears to smiles is much easier. These smiles reflect two sources of happiness. Not only has the basic problem been solved, but your baby will also have gained additional evidence that you care about him and can be trusted to help.

Fortunately, babies don't spend all their time crying. They also spend good portions of their days feeling happy and loved. Signs have a role to play here, too. When a child learns to label a smiling child at the park with the *happy* sign, or a scene in a book of a father and son hugging with the *love* sign, that child is demonstrating the development of the second talent—recognizing the emotions of others. Research shows that this skill is a critical step in the development of sympathy, empathy, and self-control, three emotional abilities all parents want their children to have and that pay off handsomely as children begin forging friendships.

If recognizing another's emotions is step one, knowing how to help is step two. Signing provides a window into the development of this important component, as well. Seventeen-month-old Kara provided us with a good example:

One morning as children were arriving at the UC Davis center, seventeen-month-old Kara saw her friend Levi begin crying as his mother tried to leave. After a moment, Kara turned to her own mom, pointed to Levi, and signed sad. *"Yes, Kara, Levi is feeling sad this morning," replied her mother. Kara then walked over to Levi and signed* fish *while eyeing him with obvious concern. Why? Because when she herself was sad, a teacher would often take her to feed the fish to cheer her up. Kara had not only understood Levi's problem, she was also suggesting a solution!*

Kara's behavior demonstrates how important it is to teach children about negative as well as positive emotions. It also shows clearly how signing can reveal a level of emotional sophistication that otherwise would remain hidden.

First Metaphors

One of the most creative ways we use language is to point out similarities between things, similarities that strike us as especially informative, beautiful, or even funny. "His face was an open book." "My love is like a red, red rose." Such parallels are called *metaphors* or *similes*. This kind of creativity represents the poet in us all. You may be surprised, as we were, to learn how early it begins.

As your baby goes on his merry way, picking up information, he inevitably ends up noticing intriguing parallels. And what do babies do when they notice interesting similarities? They simply borrow a sign from an object the present item resembles, smile expectantly, and wait to be congratulated on their remarkable insight. Thus, the earliest form of metaphor is born.

An evening stroll through the park was the occasion for a particularly nice example. According to the father of sixteen-month-old Lucy, the family had just come back from a weekend camping trip, where Lucy had been impressed by the stars and the moon. Having lived most of her short life in a city apartment, she had never before encountered the majesty of the nighttime sky. As Lucy had swung slowly in a hammock nestled in her father's arms, he had leisurely shown her two simple signs, one for *stars* and one for *moon*. It had just seemed a natural way to keep a sweet moment from ending too soon. As a veteran signer, Lucy caught on right away.

The Baby Signs Program in Action

A Fish Tale

Fifteen-month-old Brandon was settling into his seat for his first airplane ride when he looked toward the window and began smacking his lips enthusiastically. "You see a fish?" asked his mom as she followed his gaze. But it was raining quite hard, and all she could see was water rushing down the window beside his seat. Nevertheless, Brandon was insistent and continued to sign even more vehemently—*fish, fish, FISH!* Suddenly the mystery was solved as his mom looked at the window with different eyes. "Oh! I bet you're telling us it looks like our aquarium at home!" said his mom with amazement. "You're absolutely right! That's where fishies live!" Brandon's response? A big, satisfied grin.

It was the following evening back home, however, that occasioned Lucy's metaphor. As they were on their routine stroll through the small city park near their apartment, Lucy signed *moon* and turned expectant eyes toward her father. "The moon, Lucy? But I don't see the moon." When Lucy repeated the sign after another hundred yards or so, her father took a second look. This time it was clear what Lucy was proudly pointing out—the old-fashioned, wrought-iron streetlights they had both seen so many times before but had scarcely noticed. With their rounded globes and bright white lights, they did indeed resemble the moon. Her dad's description of this episode conveys one of the indirect benefits of signs: "It may seem weird to say it, but when Lucy did that, she actually taught me something important. Bring fresh eyes to even an old place, and you may be surprised by what you see."

Other babies have shown similar creativity: eleven-month-old Cady calling the broccoli on her plate a *flower*, eighteen-month-old Elizabeth calling the long-hosed vacuum cleaner an *elephant*, sixteen-month-old Austin using the *monkey* sign to describe a particularly hairy young man, and seventeen-month-old Carlos describing a trip through the car wash as *wind* and *rain*. Research from many laboratories in addition to our own indicates that the very availability of a label, be it a sign or a word, spurs a baby on to be even more watchful of the things around him.

Sign Sentences

All done and *drink.*
Where and *kitty?*
Big and *doggie!*
More and *cookie!*
—Kristen, age fourteen months

There's no doubt that a single sign—such as *more,* for example—conveys important information. But there's also no denying that the combination *more* plus *cookie* is even clearer. Babies seem to know this intuitively, and for that reason, every human child eventually does the hard work of learning how to string two symbols together, and the first sentences are born.

The appearance of these tiny sentences is a milestone in a baby's life as important to language researchers as the first word. Although they sound simple enough to us, these two-symbol combinations are thought to signal a quantum leap in the cognitive skills, especially memory, at the baby's command. They also enable the baby to become an even more effective communicator, reducing everyone's frustration and adding enormously to the pleasure of social interactions. Clearly, the earlier a baby can make this leap, the better.

When can this remarkable transition be expected? The traditional answer to this question is at about twenty months, with many babies waiting until their third year. But doesn't that make little Kristen's performance pretty impressive? Here she is, only fourteen months old and already well on her way to conveying more complex messages. In fact, Kristen's performance is one we have come to expect from signing babies. With an arsenal of signs at their disposal, they simply don't have to wait until they are able to say lots of words in order to start using sentences. The need to communicate is there, the signs are available, and the babies simply do what comes naturally; they combine signs with signs or signs with words. Voilà! Sentences!

So Kristen, highly motivated to get more milk, find the kitty, call her mother's attention to the scary dog, and eat another cookie, formed two-sign sentences to get her messages across. On other occasions she took advantage of the few words she did know, combining these with a sign or two. By fourteen months Kristen already had at her command the intellectual skills necessary to create sentences. This is a full six months earlier than is typically expected.

Kristen is not alone. Baby after baby in our studies has charmed his parents with little sign sentences. Babies are clearly much smarter than many give them credit for. What's more, the practice these babies get in

Typical Sign Combinations

Once children are off and running with signs, they often begin to use them in combination, either with other signs or with words. Here are a few favorites from our research files:

Sign-Sign Combinations

- *More* and *drink*:
  Twenty-two-month-old Portia,
  to say that the elephant was drinking at his trough for a
  second time.
- *All done* and *light*:
  Seventeen-month-old James,
  to say that Christmas lights
  had gone out.
- *Where* and *monkey*:
  Fifteen-month-old Leanne,
  to describe a gorilla's retreat
  into the cave in the zoo enclosure.

Sign-Word Combinations

- "More" and *slide*:
  Fifteen-month-old Jacob, to ask
  to go down the slide again.
- *Cookie* and "mine!":
  Seventeen-month-old Vivian,
  to make clear to her playmate that
  the cookie was hers.
- *Hat* and "Daddy":
  Sixteen-month-old Andrew,
  to label his dad's bicycle helmet.

combining signs with signs, and signs with words, actually makes the transition to word combinations that much easier. Babies also frequently combine signs with words. What is interesting about such combinations from a linguist's standpoint is that they indicate that a baby views these two types of symbols as equivalent to each other. To signing babies, it doesn't matter what kind of symbol is used, only that a message is successfully communicated.

The signs *more*, *all done*, and *where* seem to be especially popular in early signed sentences. There's a very good reason for that. These three signs, like their vocal counterparts, are particularly easy to combine with lots of different items. Everything from buttons to bows can disappear (*all done/gone*), be hard to find (*where?*), and be desired again (*more*). Other signs, especially descriptors, work in a similar way. Lots of things can be *hot* or *cold*, *little* or *big*, *in* or *out*. Remember this when you are choosing signs to teach your baby. Having a few of these signs in his repertoire will definitely increase the chance he'll be able to use signs to practice making sentences.

Potty Training with the Baby Signs Program

According to the American Academy of Pediatrics, a critical requirement for toilet training success is the ability of the child to *purposefully* signal that she needs to go potty. This recommendation has traditionally been interpreted as a need to

---

The Baby Signs Program in Action

It Works!

Not long after we began testing our potty training materials, we heard from Deanna, the mother of Adam, age thirty months, and Ashton, aged nine months. "I am so excited! We had been focusing on training Adam when we suddenly noticed that Ashton was imitating the potty sign, too. Here's what happened. Not really believing Ashton understood what it was all about, we started sitting him on the potty seat a few times a day just to get him used to the idea. Now he signs when he needs to go and is successfully pooping and peeing in the potty! We would never have thought to train Ashton so early—although my mom said I was trained by one year. I guess I should have listened! We are so glad we were a part of the field-test group. We love the Baby Signs potty training program!"

wait until a child can at least say the word *potty*—a milestone that many children won't reach until they are well past age two.

That's where signs come in! By combining the magic of signing with a commonsense plan, our new Baby Signs potty training program makes it not only possible but *easy* for potty training to be completed between twelve and twenty-four months—over a year earlier than the current average of thirty-seven months!

Why should earlier training be a goal? Because the trend toward later and later training clearly benefits the diaper industry but is *not* good for children, families, or the environment. When we took a close look at potty training at various ages, here's what we learned about early training (before age two). Early training

- is less likely to involve power struggles because it precedes the "terrible twos," when oppositional behavior becomes a problem;
- is easier because the habit of eliminating in a diaper isn't as thoroughly ingrained;
- is better for children because it decreases health problems like serious constipation, urinary tract infections, and bacterial infections (spread by hands in diapers that then touch toys);
- is better for children because it avoids feelings of shame that develop after age two;
- was the norm (completion by eighteen months) until the disposable diaper was invented in the early 1960s;
- is better for families because it saves money; and
- is *much* better for the environment!

With more than 7.25 billion pounds of disposable diapers going into American landfills every year—and with each diaper taking up to five hundred years to decompose (if it ever does)—it's definitely time for a "change"!

Does our program work? You bet it does! We know because we have tested it with families across the country with great success. From the parents in our research we've learned that one secret to its success lies in our use of a train theme ("All aboard the potty train!") in the resources we provide to help excite children about using the potty. It's with this theme in mind that we laid out the four phases of the program, which we summarize briefly here.

> Before the disposable diaper was invented, 92 percent of American children were completely potty trained by eighteen months. Today the average age is thirty-seven months—and, unfortunately, climbing.

Phase 1: Laying the Tracks

Before a train can go anywhere, there have to be train tracks—and the potty train is no exception. The goal of this stage is to lay those tracks by gently initiating *yourself* into the world of potty training starting as early as when your child is six months old. But don't worry if your child is older. The program still works like a charm!

1. **Educate yourself about potty training.** An important first step is what you are doing right now—educating yourself about potty training so that you know, at least in general terms, what lies ahead. Doing so will help reduce much of your anxiety.

2. **Incorporate signing into daily life.** You're also already working on this step. Because using signs is part of the program, getting your child used to signing is helpful.

3. **Observe your baby's signals and schedule.** Start now noticing how your particular child behaves just before she goes in her diaper, and use these signals to figure out the typical times during the day when

eliminating is most likely to happen. Once potty training is actually under way, this knowledge will help you time trips to the potty when they are most likely to result in success.

Potty

Phase 2: Pulling Slowly Out of the Station

A key word here is *slowly*. The goal of this stage, which can start as early as nine to twelve months, is to gently initiate your child into the world of potty training.

1. **Introduce five potty-time signs.** Don't worry if you didn't have a chance to start signing before this point; simply start now. We recommend these signs: *potty*, *more*, *all done*, *wash*, and *good job*. For example, show your child the potty sign when you notice him going in his diaper and when you change him, saying something like "Looks like you went *potty* in your diaper!" Your goal is to help your child begin connecting the sign with the word and with peeing and pooping.

More

All Done

2. **Buy a potty chair.** Once it's home, have your child decorate it so that she starts off with a positive attitude. Encourage your child to sit on it, too—either with or without a diaper—without any expectation of success.

Wash

3. **Introduce a few routine potty visits.** The idea is for visits to the potty to become just "something we always do." Good times might include after waking

Good Job

up, after meals, and before naps and bedtime. Don't worry if nothing happens.

4. **Make sure potty time is fun!** No parent can potty train a child who doesn't *want* to be trained, so find ways to inspire your child to cooperate. That's what being "emotionally ready" means. How? Encourage her to watch potty-time DVDs (like our All Aboard the Potty Train DVD) that promote identifying with and imitating the characters; read books and sing songs with her while she's sitting on the potty; consider stickers or other small rewards to celebrate success. Make potty time a time your child looks forward to because it signals important one-on-one time with someone she loves.

Phase 3: Picking Up Speed

With potty training having been *gently* introduced, the next step is to focus with considerably greater intensity on potty training.

1. **Decide when to begin this more intensive phase.** Because this phase requires lots of one-on-one time with your child, be sure to target a week or more when you are free to do so or when you have reliable partners to help.

2. **Establish a full potty schedule.** To maximize the chance of success, use your baby's signals and typical peeing and pooping schedule to guide you. And never ask your child if he needs to go potty. Instead, simply announce, "It's time to go potty." Don't expect success right off the bat. Remember, a well-ingrained habit of eliminating in a diaper is difficult to break.

3. **Continue modeling the potty signs.** Your goal is for your child to eventually be able to alert you when he needs to go potty using either the sign or the word, so continuing to reinforce the connection is important.

4. **Introduce cloth training pants.** In sharp contrast to today's highly absorbent diapers, cloth pants will help your child become conscious of the uncomfortable consequences of not using the potty.

5. **Expect accidents!** Accidents are inevitable, so be as prepared as you can be—with plastic pants over the training pants, extra clothes, plastic covers for chairs, etc. It's great to have your child help you clean up the mess, but *never* get angry or shame her!

Phase 4: Full Speed Ahead!

The goal of this phase is to help your child move closer and closer toward total independence. Here are some milestones along the way.

1. **Detecting the need to go potty.** The connections between eliminating, signing, and sitting on the potty will gradually grow stronger until, eventually, the sensation of having to go will lead naturally to using the sign (or word) to let you know he needs to go potty. Be patient—it *will* happen!

2. **Pulling pants down and up.** Once motor skills improve sufficiently, your child will be able to pull her own pants down at the beginning and up at the end.

3. **Learning to wipe.** Third, with your guidance, your child will learn to wipe himself properly and flush the toilet.

4. **Washing hands independently.** Fourth, your child will be able to wash her hands independently—even reminding you to do so if you happen to forget!

5. **Moving from potty chair to toilet.** And last, your child will make the transition from potty chair to regular toilet (using a potty seat to reduce the opening)—and if your child is a boy, from sitting down to standing up. This is where daddies and big brothers can come in handy!

Congratulations! You've met the challenge of potty training, and in doing so before age two, you've saved money, avoided the battle of wills so typical with children over two, and personally prevented two thousand or more diapers from harming the environment!

Off and Running—in Different Directions

Once a baby learns to walk, there's no telling exactly where he will go or what path he will take to get there. Set two babies down in the middle of a park, and one may head off toward the swings while the other may be content to meander through the dandelions. Every baby is different. In this way the adventure of learning signs is no different from the adventure of learning to walk. Every baby brings to the signing experience her own developmental history, her own interest in communication, and her own style of interacting with the world. We have seen signs being used in all the different ways described—to sharpen attention to the world, to express feelings, to focus on similarities, to begin the challenge of producing sentences. However, individual differences reign supreme in this arena as in any other, with each baby using signs in a way that suits him best.

CHAPTER 6

From Signs to Speech

Nathaniel's big sister had so much fun teaching him signs that she was really disappointed to see them go. But go they did, slowly at first, but then it seemed as though two or three would disappear every week. By the time he was twenty-two months old, the only sign he still used was monkey—*mainly because he loved hopping around scratching under his arms like a gorilla.*

—Lisa, mother of two-year-old Nathaniel

AS MUCH FUN AS THE SIGNING EXPERIENCE IS FOR EVERYONE, we certainly don't want hearing children growing up using signs *instead of* learning to talk. Fortunately, as we pointed out earlier, our research has proved that there's nothing to worry about on this count. In fact, the experience of using signs actually speeds up the process. To understand why this is so, it's important to remember that, just as crawling is a natural stage on the way to learning to walk, using signs actually represents a natural and very important stage in the development of a child's knowledge of the world in general and communication in particular.

We describe signs as a "natural stage" of development because it has so much in common with what the famous Swiss psychologist Jean Piaget called *sensorimotor development.* By very carefully observing his own three children, Piaget proved that the bulk of a baby's intellectual "work" during the first year involves learning to interact with objects (the *motor* component), to observe the results of those actions (the *sensory* component), and to organize all this information into an ever more sophisticated database. Signs, because they are action based (e.g., opening and closing the hands) and relate directly to something perceived by the senses (a book), represent sensorimotor achievements. But what's even more impressive, encouraging a child to use signs to communicate helps that child make the next leap, the one Piaget felt was the cornerstone of all intellectual development yet to come—the use of symbols. When we help babies discover that opening and closing the hands can "stand for" (symbolize) the book itself for purposes of communication, we are providing valuable preparation for future development, not only of language, but also of all the other domains that rely on symbols—imagining, drawing, reading, and thinking.

That's how using signs helps children in the big scheme of things. But it's important to remember that the experience also helps in ways that are much more specific to the challenge of learning to talk.

A Dress Rehearsal for Talking

When your baby brings you a book and begins naming animals with signs, she is showing you how much signs have already taught her about language. Her eagerness to label animals shows you how excited she is about the whole business of communicating now that she can actively participate, and how much she enjoys doing so with the people around her. Her ability to label the animals correctly also shows you how much she has already learned about the world—like what makes one animal a zebra and another a horse. This interaction also shows you that your baby already understands what symbols are all about—that one thing (a sign) can stand for another thing (an animal). These are all critical pieces of the jigsaw puzzle of language that the experience of using signs helps children put together at remarkably young ages. Without signs to signal all this, you might appreciate that she can point to things when asked and that she likes to cuddle—but that's about it.

Interactions like these teach your baby important lessons, too. The successful use of signs like *zebra*, *monkey*, *lion*, and *tiger* make it clear to him that he is correct about lots of things he has suspected. He is right that the animals in the book do belong to the categories he thought ("That is a lion!"), that symbols do function to get this information across, that naming things does make you smile, and that reading books is a great way to learn more about the things you are interested in—as

> When a baby successfully uses a sign to communicate, she gains knowledge about words, concepts, and the process of communicating that are fundamental to learning to talk.

well as to cuddle. At the same time, your enthusiastic response is providing him with more food for thought. Your conversation about the animals provides models of how words should be said, whole sentences to help him practice comprehension skills, new concepts to ponder, and the knowledge that you think he is pretty wonderful. In short, a single book-reading interaction like this is a gold mine for both of you. Of course, the same gains would have resulted had your baby used the words *zebra* and *lion*. It's just that it would have been a shame to wait another six months until he could.

Understanding the complexity of language helps us to appreciate the difficulty children have in learning words and to recognize the important role that signs can play. Babies are a lot smarter than most of us think, and using signs not only allows them to show us but also allows them to be understood—which is really what all of us want from language and from one another.

Why Your Baby Wants to Talk

As the pieces of the language puzzle fall into place one by one, helped along by signs, children are rapidly and irresistibly drawn toward the final piece—learning to say words. You'll notice we've used the phrase *irresistibly drawn* to describe the relationship between children and vocal language. What we want to convey is the magnetic pull of vocal language for every human child. All over the world, from Tokyo to Borneo, toddlers learn to talk, although the final product certainly differs from culture to culture. What stays the same is the use of complex patterns of vocal sounds to convey complex messages from person to person. No culture has ever been found, no matter how isolated from the rest of us, that didn't share this human capacity. For the world's toddlers, including those who've had the added benefit of signing, simply nothing will stop them from learning to talk!

But how can we be sure that children who communicate effectively with signs won't be so content with them that they lose their motivation to learn words? Don't children, like the rest of us, believe the old adage "If it ain't broke, don't fix it"? No, they don't—at least not when it comes to communicating with those around them. The reason is simple. As babies grow older their horizons expand and their needs change. And with these changes comes a strong desire for more sophisticated ways of communicating. As we pointed out earlier, signing is to talking as crawling is to walking. It is simply a natural step along the way.

In what ways do babies' needs change? Think about the new places, people, activities, and ideas babies encounter after their first two years of life. Together, these provide powerful incentives for babies to move toward speech.

New Places to Go

The older your child gets, the less likely she is to stay in one place for long. Her curiosity takes her around corners, up stairs, and into new rooms. At the same time, as a parent you are becoming increasingly secure that she need not be under your watchful eye absolutely every moment. So your child enjoys a new freedom to explore the nooks and crannies of her world.

What many of these new places have in common is that your child no longer can see you, and you can no longer see her. But that doesn't mean she doesn't still want to tell you things. Putting yourself in your child's place, you can quickly see the problem. As any person with a hearing impairment can tell you, the usefulness of sign language disappears when folks aren't face to face. But sounds, on the other hand, can be heard—even shouted—from room to room. So, as signers start to move farther and farther afield, learning the words behind the signs takes on an urgency not felt when everyone could be counted on to stay in one place.

New Faces to Meet

Greater mobility and maturity also mean that your child is destined to meet more and more new people along his way. These may be other families in the park or at the pool. They may be cashiers or other shoppers at the grocery store, who now talk directly to him rather than just to you. They may be the additional playmates who get added to his daycare group once he's graduated from the infant room. As his circle of friends widens, he will more frequently encounter people who don't use signs.

Some signs, it's true, will always be useful. For example, no matter what your age, an index finger brought to the lips continues to signal *quiet* and standing with your hands outstretched and palms up translates into the words "I don't know" or "Where?" But most signs will inevitably drop out in favor of the symbol system shared more widely—vocal words. All these new conversation partners, then, provide another strong incentive for your growing child to learn the words behind the signs.

New Games to Play

Getting older also means that your child will become increasingly skilled at using her body, particularly her hands, to explore and have fun in the world. There are finger paints to spread around, crayons to color with, puzzles to put together, ladders to climb, and bikes to ride. Each of these activities tends to keep hands pretty busy, making signs less and less convenient to produce. Of course, we still take time out to wave *bye-bye* pretty much regardless of what we're doing. But spoken words gain an edge over signs that they didn't have when your child was less dependent on her hands for a good time.

New Things to Say

To a fifteen-month-old, simply telling you that he sees a butterfly is a magnificent feat. In such cases a single symbol or two, be they signs or words, will suffice. However, as children grow intellectually, gathering more and more information about the world around them, the ideas they want to get across become much more complicated. What interests a child at that point is not just the fact that he sees the butterfly, but that this butterfly is like the one he saw yesterday, or that he knows it came from a cocoon, or that its colors remind him of Halloween.

Except for children whose parents are capable of teaching them to be fluent in ASL, ideas of this complexity are simply not what signs are for. Signs from the Baby Signs program are tremendously effective labels for the common objects of the younger baby's world, but by the time a child knows about *yesterday*, *cocoons*, and *Halloween*, it's time to move on. Your child will automatically sense when this time has come and will eagerly conquer the verbal vocabulary he needs.

The Transition to Speech

Even though we often get the impression that babies make great intellectual leaps between the time they go to bed at night and the time they get up in the morning, when it comes to the shift from signs to words, the process is usually gradual. Once in a while, it's true, we'll see a word appear out of nowhere, and—poof!—the sign is gone. But in the vast majority of cases, the transition proceeds more slowly.

A good example is eighteen-month-old Megan's gradual shift from her *toothbrush* sign to her version of the word ("too-bus").

- **Thirteen to eighteen months:** Megan uses the sign exclusively, especially when she joins her mother in the bathroom in the morning.
- **Eighteen months:** Megan occasionally begins to mutter something that sounds vaguely like the word, always pairing it with the sign. Her parents have trouble understanding what she is saying and depend on the sign as a translation.
- **Nineteen months:** The sign and the word become equal partners, Megan using them together pretty consistently.

- **Twenty months:** Megan confidently uses the word in all but a few special circumstances (described at the end of the chapter). For Megan, the transition is complete!

Gone but Not Forgotten

Let's jump to the final stage of the transition to speech, the point where the word becomes firmly entrenched. Even after your baby is confidently using the word behind a sign, chances are that he'll still have the sign available to use in special circumstances, at least for a while. Think about your own use of signs. Have you completely stopped waving *good-bye* just because you have the word? No. You automatically recognize occasions when the sign works better than (or better with) the word. Similarly, the following situations motivate signers to revive their signs and put them to work. It's quite possible that, as your child transitions from signs to speech, you'll find other situations to add to the list.

To Clarify a Message

Learning how to say words clearly enough for adults to understand is a real challenge. A toddler may know that "kikiki" means kitty, or "tur" means turtle, but that doesn't mean anyone else does. Children with signs spontaneously use them as clarification when they see a confused look on someone's face. And it works! "Ohhh! 'um-kee' means monkey! I see!" Similarly, Megan, whose transition to words we described earlier, used a sign to clarify her word for toothbrush when she was visiting her grandmother. Although her mother knew that "too-bus" meant "toothbrush," her grandmother did not. The sign made the meaning clear.

When Food Is in the Way

A mouth that's full of food is a real obstacle to intelligible speech. No doubt you can recall times when someone has asked you to pass the salt just as you were stuffing a forkful of potato into your mouth. Looking around and not seeing it,

How Long Signs Last Depends on Many Things

Q: *How soon after my baby learns a sign will he start trying to say the word?*

A: The answer, as usual, is that it all depends. If the sign is substituting for a relatively easy word like *ball* or *more*, the word may appear quickly. On the other hand, if the word is long and complicated, like *elephant* or *butterfly*, the sign is likely to stick around longer.

It also depends on a baby's choice of strategy. Some children use signs to free them to work on learning words for *other* things. These babies tend to hold on to their signs for quite a while, using them to increase the number of things they can talk about. Other babies seem to use signs to speed up learning the word a sign stands for. In these cases, the word appears relatively quickly. The logic lies in the fact that the more frequently a baby uses a sign, the more often adults respond by saying the word, thereby providing more opportunities for the child to learn it. And, of course, some babies use *both* strategies!

up come your hands and shoulders, and you shrug to say "I don't know where it is." The gesture has rescued you from your dilemma. Signing children use their signs in the same way. Max, for example, already had a mouthful of crackers when his caregiver at childcare passed by with the cracker box. Not willing to let her get away without another portion for himself, Max was able to bypass his mouth altogether by reviving his *more* sign. He had been saying the word *more* for several weeks but could still fall back on the sign when the need arose.

For Emphasis

Have you ever said, "Naughty!" while simultaneously shaking your index finger vigorously at your dog or shouted, "Out!" while pointing to the door? There are times, it seems, when words alone simply aren't strong enough. Babies and toddlers apparently feel this way too. Take twenty-month-old Karen, for example.

She had finished her cup of apple juice and was calling to her mother from across the kitchen with the words "Mo dink!" But her mother, busy on the phone, wasn't paying any attention. Karen's solution? She moved right into her mother's face and repeated "Mo dink! Mo dink! Mo dink!" quite loudly, each time pairing it with her old *more* sign. And she did so with great gusto, tapping her fingertips together forcefully as if to say, ". . . and I want it now!" Such creativity with signs seems to come naturally to babies and adults alike.

The Baby Signs Program in Action

Educating Dolly

Isabella was a great signer until she turned fourteen months and was so "into words" that she stopped using signs altogether. So it went for a whole year, Isabella learning more and more words until signs were only a vague memory—or so it seemed until one day Isabella, now twenty-six months old, sat down to play with her favorite doll. With her mother looking on open-mouthed, Isabella proceeded to give her doll a signing lesson. "Birdie," said Isabella while flapping her own arms, the baby-friendly sign she had used so long ago. Then, repeating the word, she grasped the doll's arms and moved them up and down. The lesson continued a few more times, Isabella patiently demonstrating the sign and never seeming to mind that her pupil was unimpressed!

When Words Can't (or Shouldn't) Be Heard

Even though words have the advantage of being "shoutable," sometimes the noise level is just too high to make even shouting effective. At such times, signs are particularly handy. We've heard of former signers resurrecting old signs for this reason at football games, at circuses, and in shopping malls. The opposite situation, where silence prevails and talking is inappropriate, also has motivated children to replace words they know with old signs. James, a twenty-four-month-old with an impressive vocal vocabulary, rediscovered the usefulness of several signs in church. Another toddler, who frequently visited the university library with her student mother, routinely used her *book* sign even though she'd known the word for months. And then there's the *potty* sign. Both parents and children love having a subtle way to communicate unobtrusively about the need to visit the bathroom.

When Little Sister or Brother Comes Along

There's one other reason why older children sometimes still use their signs. Many families have reported that the arrival of a younger brother or sister keeps the older sibling's enthusiasm high. The opportunity to team up with parents to teach the new baby how to communicate is simply hard to resist—especially because signing is inherently lots of fun for everyone.

A Legacy of Love That Lasts a Lifetime

Perhaps the most important ways in which signs are not forgotten have nothing to do with opportunities to make the signs themselves. Yes, it's true that we've found long-term benefits to language and intelligence from using signs during the first two years of life. But the importance of each of these effects pales in comparison to the long-term emotional benefits we've heard described by thousands of parents. Babies who sign learn very early in life that their thoughts and feelings matter and will be listened to. As a result of being effective in the world, they develop positive attitudes toward others—and toward themselves. They discover that learning is fun, that the world is a marvelously interesting place, and that it's enormously rewarding to share one's fascinating discoveries with those one loves.

While more difficult to test in a laboratory, these emotional benefits will be obvious as you watch your child move through the signing stage into the wider world of words—and then through the maze of experiences that make each child's life unique. With the wonderful ballast provided by these early doses of love and understanding, your child's chances of safe passage through these experiences will be strengthened, and your own satisfaction at having helped your child toward emotional happiness will be immense. In other words, the gift of signs is a gift that lasts a lifetime.

APPENDIX A

Signing and Childcare: A Wonderful Partnership

When I first started signing with my child, I was worried that my efforts wouldn't pay off because she was in childcare so much of the time. But I quickly realized that she was still easily learning the signs and that her ability to sign was making the times we were together even better! Her teachers were very impressed with her ability to communicate, and now all the kids in the center are signing. Even the few who can already talk think it's great fun.

—Mother of fifteen-month-old Jasmine

LIKE JASMINE'S MOM, MANY WORKING PARENTS WONDER whether they can take advantage of the Baby Signs program because they are away from their baby for a good part of the day. The answer is a resounding "Yes!" We know this is true because we've heard success stories like this from so many working moms and dads.

Children in full-time care spend significantly more time with their parents than with outsiders. Who is it, after all, who provides the evening meal and bath, cuddles to read a bedtime book, responds to middle-of-the-night calls for help, and spends weekends dealing with every kind of need? In fact, because so much quality time is spent with parents, research shows that even infants and toddlers who are in full-time childcare still keep their parents number one in their hearts.

As a result, babies of working parents are just as keen to learn what their parents have to teach, imitate their behaviors, and open lines of communication—a perfect formula for successful signing!

As Jasmine's mother pointed out, signing is a real gift to working parents because it makes the time you do spend together more peaceful and satisfying. For example, signs work great during those hectic early-morning dressing and eating routines when you are trying to get everybody ready and out the door on time. Signs can also be particularly helpful at the end of the day to reduce feelings of frustration that can arise so easily when everyone is tired.

> Even babies in full-time childcare learn signs easily from their parents. What's more, signing makes the time parents and children do spend together more peaceful and satisfying.

Speaking of being tired, don't forget that bedtime signs—like the *sleep/bed* sign—can be a huge help by enabling babies to actually let parents know that they are tired and ready for sleep. Being able to communicate such an important message is a real boon to both parent and child because everyone avoids the chaos that often ensues when a child moves into the overtired realm.

In other words, by clarifying your baby's needs, signs help mealtime, bathtime, and bedtime routines go more smoothly. They help you reconnect and share your experiences after a long day apart and help turn typically stressful times into warm and precious moments. Whether you're a working parent or not, signs simply make day-to-day life a lot more fun.

The Baby Signs Program in Childcare

There's another side, however, to the working parent and signing story. As more and more parents discover the joys of signing with their babies, the good news is inevitably spreading beyond the home and into childcare settings. Why?

Because the same benefits experienced within the family also hold true wherever small and large groups of babies are cared for.

In fact, many signing parents these days specifically seek out childcare centers where the Baby Signs program is an integral part of daily life. However, if your childcare provider hasn't yet "signed on" to signing, try sharing the following list of benefits revealed in research conducted at the Center for Child and Family Studies at UC Davis. The data revealed that:

- Reduces frustration and tears, thereby making classrooms more peaceful and children less anxious
- Decreases biting and other aggressive behaviors that occur when children don't have words
- Builds trust between babies and caregivers because babies are confident their needs will be met
- Motivates caregivers to pay closer attention to children and, therefore, to respond to their needs more quickly and more appropriately
- Promotes positive emotional development by enabling children to express emotions and feelings, including empathy
- Provides a universal language so that children and caregivers who don't speak the same language can still communicate

Who wouldn't want their child to be in an environment where all these wonderful benefits are available?

So, if your childcare program doesn't yet use signing in the classroom, by all means encourage the providers to visit www.babysigns.com and learn how easy it is to incorporate the Baby Signs program

> **The Baby Signs Program in Action**
>
> **International Relations!**
> Two toddlers, one from Israel and one from Taiwan, were best friends at the UC Davis Center for Child and Family Studies. Despite the fact that neither one spoke or understood the other's native language, they still found a way to enjoy a book together. Sitting on the floor with the book between them, one would turn the page, point at a picture, and the other would make the sign!

into small and large childcare settings. And remember, there's strength in numbers. Find out whether other families with children in the center are also signing at home, and work together to make your case.

If Your Childcare Provider Already Uses Signs

Maybe you're one of the lucky parents whose child attends a program that already uses signing in the classroom. That's wonderful, not only because it means that your child will receive support for signing even when away from home, but also because of the many benefits already discussed.

Even if you're one of these lucky families, however, it's natural to worry that other people won't understand what your child is trying to communicate when she uses a sign. Although this does happen, the instances are far fewer than you might think. Three factors help adults—assuming they are watching for signs—successfully interpret many of the signs babies use:

1. The situation often makes it fairly easy to figure out what a baby is signing. A baby looking longingly at a bowl of Goldfish crackers while swishing his hands is probably using his *fish* sign to request some "fish" for himself.
2. Many signs resemble the items they stand for or the actions typically done with them. Examples include *ball, banana, book, comb, hat, ice cream, pacifier, rain, shampoo, spider, toothbrush,* and *turtle.*
3. A surprising number of useful signs are actually "conventional" signs, meaning that even adults use them now and again. Think about *all done, baby, cold, down, drink, eat, love, monkey, noise, sad, sleep, stop,* and many more.

What if Signs at Home Are Different?

Q: *My baby already knows a few signs. I would like to enroll him in a center where signs are used, but I worry that the signs they use may look different from the ones that my son has learned. Will he be confused?*

A: Even families who use only ASL signs are likely to find differences between signs at home and signs in the classroom. The reason is that not all ASL signs are standardized. They can vary from place to place and from one signing dictionary to another. If such a situation arises, simply let your son's caregivers know what sign he prefers so they can watch for it. Remember, caregivers and babies work out such differences all the time when it comes to early words, and no one worries. Caregivers quickly learn each baby's idiosyncratic ways of signing just as they learn their idiosyncratic ways of vocalizing. If you want to, it's also fine to switch the sign you use at home to the one used in the classroom. Babies catch on quickly.

Tips for Educating Caregivers

No matter who is caring for your child while she is away from you, it is important to let those individuals know that you are encouraging your child to use signs. Unless they are aware that this is the case, there's a good chance that they will be oblivious to your child's attempts to communicate with signs, and both caregiver and baby will miss out on the many benefits signing brings.

Over the years we've had a chance to talk with both parents and childcare professionals about ways to get caregivers on board with signing. Below are some of the creative ideas they've shared with us:

- Let caregivers borrow this book. Mark sections you think would be especially helpful—like the ten tips for success in Chapter 3 and the benefits of signing described both here and in Chapter 1.
- If your child is cared for in your home, provide access to the free DVD with the Baby Signs dictionary. If you use a center or family childcare, consider lending the DVD for a short period of time.
- Photocopy pages of the dictionary that include signs your baby knows or is working on, circle the relevant signs, and give them to the person or people caring for your child. Don't forget to provide periodic updates!
- Provide caregivers with a commercially available reference guide that includes simple sign illustrations.
- If your child uses lots of signs, consider videotaping yourself doing the signs the way your child does. This is particularly practical in the case of individuals who care for your child in your home (like Grandma or a nanny).

And finally, if caregivers express concern that signing will slow your child's verbal development, provide them with

---

The Baby Signs Program in Action

Just a Gentle Reminder

Twenty-month-old Tosha needed her diaper changed, so her teacher carefully placed her on her back on the changing table. Just as she was lifting Tosha's legs high in the air to remove the old diaper, Tosha looked anxiously into her teacher's eyes and said something that sounded like "tie." "I'm sorry, but I don't understand, Tosha," said her teacher. At that, Tosha raised her hands so her teacher could see them and proceeded to stroke the back of one hand with the fingertips of the other. Her teacher immediately recognized the sign for *gentle*. "Oh, you're saying 'tight!' I'm holding your ankles too tight and it hurts. You want me to be more gentle!" responded Kathleen. Just as she did at home, Tosha was able to convey her needs and feel confident that she was, quite literally, in good hands.

a photocopy of Appendix B so that they can read about our research studies showing that the exact opposite is true.

Opening a Window for Everyone

Remember, signing provides a window into your baby's mind that anyone can look through once they understand how your child uses his signs. And what a fascinating view it is! Being able to see the world through your baby's eyes will inevitably make the relationship between your child and his caregivers richer and more satisfying to both. So, let anyone who cares for your child know which signs are important to him, and keep them abreast of his progress. Let them know how important you think it is that your baby be able to communicate with people he is exposed to on a regular basis. And if they don't already use the Baby Signs program, by all means encourage them to do so. Once caregivers are on board, they'll be eager to describe the clever ways your child is using signs during the day and share your enthusiasm about new signs as they come along at home. In short, don't let the fact that you're a working parent stop you from enjoying all the benefits of signing. With signs "on hand," everyone wins.

> The ability signing provides to see the world through your baby's eyes makes the relationship between your child and his caregivers richer and more satisfying to both.

APPENDIX B

Further Research and Readings

EVERYONE KNOWS THAT GOOD SCIENCE REQUIRES LOTS OF hard work. Our Baby Signs program research was certainly no exception. The hard work was not only on our part, however. Over our two decades of studying how hearing babies use signs (or *symbolic gestures* as we call them in our professional papers) at the University of California, Davis, we had the help of more than a hundred undergraduate and graduate students, the majority working with us for a year or more. Fortunately, good science is more than hard work. Done right, and with the right people (like our dedicated students and enthusiastic families), research is also lots of fun and enormously rewarding. That has certainly been our experience.

Our fondest hope at this point is that others will be inspired by what we have already discovered about signing with hearing babies and join us in learning more. In order to summarize all that we now know, we have chosen to highlight four of our studies, each one representative of a significant phase in our program of research. References to our other relevant papers are included in a subsequent section. We also provide a list of papers that report the work of other researchers that may be useful to understanding this important new window into the infant mind. Finally, we list useful ASL dictionaries and websites for parents who are interested in trying signs not included in our book.

Phase 1: Case Study

Linda Acredolo and Susan Goodwyn (1985). "Symbolic Gesturing in Language Development: A Case Study." *Human Development, 28:* 40–49.

This article presents the story of our first little signer, Linda's daughter Kate, who began to spontaneously create symbolic gestures when she was about twelve months old. Kate's signs were sensible gestures—like sniffing for *flower* and arms up for *big*. We then made it easy for her by modeling other simple gestures for things she was interested in and followed her progress in terms of both signing and verbal development. During the six months before words took over, Kate learned to use twenty-nine signs (thirteen of her own creation) and was able to communicate effectively about a wide variety of things. The fact that Kate's verbal development was extremely rapid (752 words at twenty-four months) provided our first solid evidence that encouraging children to use simple signs would not hinder them from learning to talk.

Phase 2: Naturalistic Observation

Linda Acredolo and Susan Goodwyn (1988). "Symbolic Gesturing in Normal Infants." *Child Development, 59:* 450–466.

Our goal in the two separate studies described in this article was to learn more about the spontaneous development of signs by infants. Was Linda's daughter alone in doing so, or were other babies just as creative? In the first study, mothers of thirty-eight seventeen-month-old infants were interviewed about their children's use of verbal and nonverbal "words." In the second study, parents of sixteen eleven-month-old infants were asked to keep records of any signlike gestures they observed their children using during the course of daily life. Diary entries continued until each child's second birthday. Both studies provided evidence that most children create at least one or two signs, and that some children, like Kate, create many. Also like Kate, the children who created lots of signs tended to excel in verbal language development. Finally, we found that parents of girls were more likely than parents of boys to report their children creating signs, and that the movements children chose to use were typically ones that made sense in some way (e.g., panting for *dog*, knob-turning gesture for *out*). Signing, in other words, was turning out to be a normal part of language development.

Phase 3: Experimental Study

Susan Goodwyn, Linda Acredolo, and Catherine Brown (2000). "Impact of Symbolic Gesturing on Early Language Development." *Journal of Nonverbal Behavior, 24:* 81–103.

In 1989 we began the most ambitious of our Baby Signs program projects. With the help of a grant from the National Institutes of Health, we designed a longitudinal study to see how purposefully encouraging babies to use signs would affect later development. To this end, 140 eleven-month-old infants were divided into three groups. These included a group of 32 infants whose parents were asked to encourage signing, a control group of infants whose parents were given no instructions about special ways to interact with their children, and a second control group (for "training effects") of infants whose parents were asked to provide lots of verbal labels to stimulate language development. All groups were found to be comparable at the beginning of the study in terms of the following factors: number of boys versus girls, number of firstborn versus later-born children, maternal and paternal education levels, family income, tendency to babble during parent-child interaction at eleven months, and number of verbal words already in their vocabularies at the beginning of the study. The study lasted two years, with 103 of the original families staying involved the entire time.

The average number of signs learned by children in the signing group was twenty (the range was ten to sixty), and no sex differences were found. Standardized tests of both receptive (ability to understand what others say) and expressive (ability to say things oneself) language development were administered at eleven, fifteen, nineteen, twenty-four, thirty, and thirty-six months.

Results demonstrated a consistent advantage for the signing babies, thereby laying to rest the most frequently voiced concern of parents—that signing might hamper learning to talk. In fact, the good news was that the signing experience actually facilitated verbal language development. What's more, the control group children, whose parents were trying hard to help them learn verbal labels, did not show a significant advantage over the nonintervention control group. This fact provides evidence that the signing children's language advantage was due specifically to the signing experience rather than just more parent-child, language-oriented interactions.

Phase 4: Long-Term Follow-Up

Linda Acredolo and Susan Goodwyn (July 2000). "The Long-Term Impact of Symbolic Gesturing During Infancy on IQ at Age 8." Paper presented at the meetings of the International Society for Infant Studies, Brighton, United Kingdom.

Whenever and wherever we presented the results of our NIH study, someone would ask whether the signing babies had continued to excel as they got older and entered elementary school. We finally decided to find out. In the summer following their second-grade year, we tracked down nineteen of the original signing babies and twenty-four of the original nonintervention control group babies. Fortunately, despite having failed to find some of the original children from each group, the two groups still did not differ from one another in the numbers of boys versus girls, number of firstborns versus later-borns, levels of maternal or paternal education, or income. The measure we chose to use to assess development was a traditional IQ test called the Wechsler Intelligence Scale for Children (WISC-III). Much to our surprise and delight, the results indicated a statistically significant 12-point advantage for the children who had been encouraged to use signs during their second year of life (the mean IQ was 114) over the children who had been in the nonintervention control group (the mean IQ was 102). In terms more relevant to daily life, the eight-year-old former signers were performing more like typical nine-year-olds, while the control children were performing just as you would expect them to at their age. The paper closes with our thoughts about why signing has this positive long-term effect on development, including both long-term cognitive and emotional effects of the early signing experience.

Phase 5: Recent Research with Special Populations

As appreciation of the importance of the earliest years of life has grown, both public and private programs have increased efforts to provide education-oriented childcare and parenting advice to low-income families and other "special circumstances" populations (e.g., foster parents, teen parents, and adoptive families). A prime example of this effort is the federally funded Early Head Start (EHS) program targeting low-income children from birth to age three.

Prompted by the remarkable results from our original NIH-funded study as well as the benefits of signing in childcare documented at UC Davis, a graduate student at UC Davis, Claire Vallotton (now Dr. Vallotton), conducted a carefully designed intervention study within the Yolo County (California) EHS program. EHS families who were encouraged to use the Baby Signs program with their children were compared to EHS families who were not using both traditional psychological assessment questionnaires (including a Parenting Stress Index) and evaluations of videotaped recordings of mother-child interactions. The results were very exciting because, in addition to language benefits, they revealed significant positive effects on the mother-child relationship. Specifically, the use of signs by families

- led to mothers perceiving their children as more "reinforcing" and "acceptable,"
- helped mothers be more "tuned in" to their children's emotions during interactions,
- increased children's attempts to communicate with their mothers,

- decreased the number of expressions of distress from children, and increased the appropriateness of mothers' responses to distress.

These results suggest that the addition of the Baby Signs program to EHS curricula for parents is an easy and effective way to improve family interactions in low-income families. Similar exciting work with low-income families is being carried out in Santiago, Chile, with funding from the Chilean government and under the guidance of Dr. Chamarrita Farkas of the Pontifica Universidad Católica de Chile.

Additional Baby Signs Research Articles from Our Lab at UC Davis

Linda Acredolo and Susan Goodwyn (1990). "Sign Language Among Hearing Infants: The Spontaneous Development of Symbolic Gestures." In *From Gesture to Language in Hearing and Deaf Children*, edited by V. Volterra and C. Erting. New York: Springer-Verlag.

Linda Acredolo and Susan Goodwyn (1990). "The Significance of Symbolic Gesturing for Understanding Language Development." In *Annals of Child Development*, edited by R. Vasta, Vol. 7, 1–42. London: Jessica Kingsley Publishers.

Susan Goodwyn and Linda Acredolo (1993). "Symbolic Gesture Versus Word: Is There a Modality Advantage for Onset of Symbol Use?" *Child Development, 64:* 688–701.

Linda Acredolo and Susan Goodwyn (1997). "Furthering Our Understanding of What Humans Understand." *Human Development, 40:* 25–31.

Susan Goodwyn and Linda Acredolo (1998). "Encouraging Symbolic Gestures: Effects on the Relationship Between Gesture and Speech." In *The Nature and Functions of Gesture in Children's Communication*, edited by J. Iverson and S. Goldin-Meadows, 61–73. San Francisco: Jossey-Bass.

Linda Acredolo, Susan Goodwyn, Karen Horobin, and Yvonne Emmons (1999). "The Signs and Sounds of Early Language Development." In *Child Psychology: A Handbook of Contemporary Issues*, edited by L. Balter and C. Tamis-LeMonda, 116–139. New York: Psychology Press.

Brie Moore, Linda Acredolo, and Susan Goodwyn (April 2001). "Symbolic Gesturing and Joint Attention: Partners in Facilitating Verbal Development." Paper presented at the Biennial Meetings of the Society for Research in Child Development, Minneapolis.

Other Professional Books and Papers Relevant to Sign Language for Hearing Children

Abrahamsen, A. (2000). "Explorations of Enhanced Gestural Input to Children in the Bimodal Period." In *The Signs of Language Revisited: An Anthology to Honor Ursula Bellugi and Edward Klima*, edited by K. Emmorey and Harlan Lane. Mahwah, NJ: LEA Publishers.

Boyatzis, C., ed. (2000). *Journal of Nonverbal Behavior, 24:* 59–174. Special Issue devoted to "Gesture and Development."

Capirci, O., Cattani, A., Rossini, P., and Volterra, V. (1998). "Teaching Sign Language to Hearing Children as a Possible Factor in Cognitive Enhancement." *Journal of Deaf Studies and Deaf Education, 3:* 135–142.

Capone, N. C., and McGregor, K. K. (2004). "Gesture Development: A Review for Clinical and Research Practices." *Journal of Speech, Language, and Hearing Research, 47:* 173–186.

Daniels, M. (2001). *Dancing with Words: Signing for Hearing Children's Literacy.* Westport, CT: Bergin & Garvey.

Daniels, M. (1996). "Seeing Language: The Effect over Time of Sign Language on Vocabulary Development in Early Childhood Education." *Child Study Journal, 26:* 193–208.

Daniels, M. (1994). "The Effects of Sign Language on Hearing Children's Language Development." *Communication Education, 43:* 291–298.

Farkas, C., and Vallotton, C. D. (August 2008). "The Baby Signs Program: Applications in Child Care Settings Across Cultures." Paper presented at the 11th Congress of the World Association of Infant Mental Health, Yokohama, Japan.

Goldin-Meadow, S., and Feldman, H. (1975). "The Creation of a Communication System: A Study of Deaf Children of Hearing Parents." *Sign Language Studies, 8:* 225–234.

Griffith, P. L. (1985). "Mode-Switching and Mode-Finding in a Hearing Child of Deaf Parents." *Sign Language Studies, 48:* 195–222.

Hall, S. S., and Weatherly, K. S. (1989). "Using Sign Language with Tracheotomized Infants and Children." *Pediatric News, 15:* 362–367.

Holmes, K. M., and Holmes, D. W. (1980). "Signed and Spoken Language Development in a Hearing Child of Hearing Parents." *Sign Language Studies, 28:* 239–254.

Iverson, J., Capirci, O., and Caselli, M. (1994). "From Communication to Language in Two Modalities." *Cognitive Development, 9:* 23–43.

Iverson, J., and Goldin-Meadows, S., eds. (1998). *The Nature and Functions of Gesture in Children's Communication,* 61–73. San Francisco: Jossey-Bass.

Marchman, V. A., and Fernald, A. (2008). "Speed of Word Recognition and Vocabulary Knowledge in Infancy Predict Cognitive and Language Outcomes in Later Childhood. *Developmental Science, 11:* 9–16.

Moore, M. (March 2007). "The Boom in Baby Signs: Of Proven Benefit for Hearing Babies . . . But What About Those Who Are Deaf?" *Deaf Life,* 33–45.

Namy, L., and Waxman, S. (1998). "Words and Gestures: Infants' Interpretations of Different Forms of Symbolic Reference." *Child Development, 69:* 295–308.

Prinz, P. M., and Prinz, E. A. (1979). "Simultaneous Acquisition of ASL and Spoken English." *Sign Language Studies, 25:* 283–296.

Vallotton, C. D. (in press). "Opening Our Minds to the Baby's Mind." *Journal of Infant Mental Health.*

Vallotton, C. D. (2008). "Signs of Emotion: What Can Preverbal Children 'Say' About Internal States?" *Journal of Infant Mental Health, 29(3):* 234–258.

Vallotton, C. D. (June 2008). "Helping Caregivers Attune to Individual Infants: Infants' and Caregivers' Use of Infant Sign Language Enhances Caregiver Responsiveness." Paper presented at Head Start's Ninth National Research Conference, Washington, D.C.

Vallotton, C. D. (August 2008). "Overcoming the Terrible Two's: Babies Change Their Caregivers' Minds and Behaviors by Using Symbolic Gestures to Communicate." Paper presented at the 11th Congress of the World Association of Infant Mental Health, Yokohama, Japan.

American Sign Language Sources

Websites

American Sign Language Browser (Michigan State): http://commtechlab.msu.edu/sites/aslweb/browser.htm

ASL Pro (University of Phoenix): http://www.aslpro.com

Dictionaries

Costello, E. (2008). *Random House Webster's American Unabridged Sign Language Dictionary*. New York: Random House Publishers.

Costello, E. (2008). *Random House Webster's Pocket American Sign Language Dictionary*. New York: Random House Publishers.

Sternberg, M. (1998). *American Sign Language Dictionary Unabridged*. New York: Collins.

Valli, C., Lott, P., Renner, D., and Hills, R. W. (2006). *The Gallaudet Dictionary of American Sign Language*. Washington, DC: Gallaudet University Press.

APPENDIX C

Baby Signs Dictionary

THIS VASTLY EXPANDED BABY SIGNS DICTIONARY IS DIVIDED
into three parts. In the first section you will find, in alphabetical order, photographs depicting 150 American Sign Language (ASL) signs as modeled by Jamie Stevens, ASL interpreter for the Deaf. The specific forms of the signs shown in the dictionary were chosen in consultation with Ms. Stevens under the guidance of the ASL Department at Columbia College, Chicago. Our goal was to pick, from the many variations used across the country, those forms most commonly used today within the United States. The resulting signs represent 150 things babies want and need to communicate about during their first two to three years—like signs for mealtime, bedtime, bathtime, feelings, and animals. (Sources for additional ASL signs are provided at the end of Appendix B.)

For those families interested in a more flexible approach, the second section of the dictionary includes photographs depicting 35 "baby-friendly" sign options as modeled by Leah Broughton. These signs, also presented in alphabetical order, provide quick and easy-to-learn alternatives created by babies themselves.

We also include the 26 signs of the ASL manual alphabet because a few of the ASL signs included in the dictionary require "finger spelling." In addition, you may want to refer to the manual alphabet when other ASL signs make use of these "hand shapes."

The following is an alphabetical listing of all signs included in the Baby Signs dictionary:

ASL Signs

Afraid	Candy	Duck
Airplane	Car	Eat
All done	Careful	Egg
Angry	Carrot	Elephant
Apple	Cat	Fan
Baby	Cereal	Fish
Ball	Cheese	Flower
Banana	Chicken	French fries
Bath	Clean up	Friend
Bear	Clock	Frog
Bed/sleep	Clothes	Fruit
Bib	Cloud	Gentle
Big	Coat	Gift
Bike	Cold	Giraffe
Bird	Comb	Girl
Blanket	Cookie	Go
Blue	Cow	Goat
Boat	Cracker	Grandma
Book	Daddy	Grandpa
Boy	Dance	Grapes
Bread	Diaper	Green
Brother	Dirty	Hair
Bubbles	Doctor	Happy
Bug	Dog	Hat
Bunny	Down	Help
Butterfly	Drink	Home

Horse	Pacifier	Spider
Hot	Pajamas	Squirrel
Hot dog	Peas	Stars
Hurt	Pig	Stop
Ice cream	Pink	Sun
In	Play	Swim
Juice	Please	Swing
Jump	Potty	Telephone
Key	Purple	Thank you
Light	Rain	Toothbrush
Lion	Red	Train
Little	Sad	Tree
Love	Shampoo	Turtle
Medicine	Share	Vegetable
Milk	Sheep	Walk
Mommy	Shoes	Want
Monkey	Sick	Wash
Moon	Sister	Watch/time
More	Sleep/bed	Water
Mouse	Slide	Where
Movie	Snow	Yellow
My/mine	Soap	Yogurt
Noise	Socks	Zebra
Orange	Song	
Outside	Spaghetti	

Baby-Friendly Signs

Afraid	Diaper	Outside
Airplane	Dog	Pig
Ball	Duck	Spider
Bib	Elephant	Stars
Big	Fish	Stop
Bird	Flower	Sun
Bubbles	Frog	Swing
Bug	Good job!	Telephone
Bunny	Horse	Train
Cereal	Hot	Wash
Chicken	Light	Where
Dance	Moon	

American Sign Language Signs

Afraid

Move hands over body as if protecting it.

Airplane

With "Y" hand, swoop hand upward like a plane flying.

All done

Starting with palms up,
turn hands over and
sweep outward.

Angry

Bend fingers while
pulling hand away
from face.

Apple

Twist bent index finger
on cheek.

Baby

Cradle arms and rock
them back and forth.

Ball

Make the shape of a ball
with hands.

Banana

Pretend index finger is a
banana and peel it.

Bath

Move fists up and down
as if scrubbing body.

Bear

Cross arms and make
clawing motion at chest.

Bed / sleep

Form pillow with one or
both hands. Tilt and rest
head on hands.

Bib

Fingerspell B-I-B and
outline the shape of a bib
on chest.

Big

With index fingers and
thumbs up, move
hands apart.

Bike

Mimic a pedaling action
with fists.

Bird

With index finger and thumb, make a beak by mouth. Open and close.

Blanket

With both hands at waist, pull imaginary blanket up over chest.

Blue

Slightly twist the right "B" hand from side to side several times.

Boat

Cup hands together and bob them forward as if in water.

Book

Make a book with
palms together.
Open and close.

Boy

With thumb and
extended fingers,
grasp the brim of an
imaginary cap.

Bread

Fingertips of right hand
slice down backside of
left hand.

Brother

Touch temple with
thumb of right "L" hand
and move down to rest
on left "L" hand.

Bubbles

Fingerspell B-U-B-B-L-E-S.
Represent rising bubbles
with rising wiggling fingers.
Then "pop open" rising
"O" hands in the air.

Bug

With thumb on nose,
bend first two fingers up
and down.

Bunny

With hand facing
backward and first two
fingers up, place hand
at side of head and
wiggle fingers.

Butterfly

Cross hands in front, link
thumbs, and flap fingers
like wings.

Candy

Twist index finger at side
of mouth.

Car

Steer imaginary steering
wheel up and down.

Careful

Strike two "K" hands
together at wrists.

Carrot

Make a fist and pretend
to chomp a carrot.

Cat

Trace imaginary cat
whiskers with thumb and
index finger.

Cereal

Using "C" hand, scoop
upward from open palm
as if scooping cereal
from a bowl.

Cheese

Place palms together
and twist as if pressing
cheese.

Chicken

Make beak with index
finger and thumb and
bring down to peck at
open palm.

Clean up

One palm swipes down the other palm as if brushing something off.

Clock

Tap back of wrist, then raise two "C" hands like imaginary clock.

Clothes

Brush open hands down chest several times.

Cloud

At forehead, both hands rotate in alternating motions.

Coat

Move thumbs of both
"A" hands down chest,
outlining lapels of a coat.

Cold

"Shiver" both fists at
shoulder level.

Comb

Run fingertips through
hair as if combing.

Cookie

Place fingertips of right
hand on left palm and
twist as if cutting with a
cookie cutter.

Cow

Twist one or both "Y" hands at temple.

Cracker

Bend one arm across chest. Tap elbow with fist of other hand.

Daddy

Tap forehead with thumb of open hand.

Dance

Swing fingertips of "V" hand rhythmically back and forth over open palm.

Diaper

Rest thumb at side of
waist. Tap thumb twice
with first two fingers.

Dirty

Place back of hand under
chin and wiggle fingers.

Doctor

Tap one "D" hand on
other wrist.

Dog

Snap fingers of one
hand. Can be followed by
patting thigh.

Down

With index finger, point down several times.

Drink

Form a cup with "C" hand. Bring to mouth.

Duck

With first two fingers and thumb, make bill by mouth. Open and close.

Eat

Touch fingertips to lips.

Egg

Tap fingers of right "H" hand on fingers of left "H" hand and move them down and apart.

Elephant

Starting at nose, trace the trunk of an elephant.

Fan

Fingerspell F-A-N, then make circles with raised index finger.

Fish

Swim one hand (or both together) forward.

Flower

Form flower bud with fingertips and touch one side of nose and then the other.

French fries

Swing "F" hands from left to right as if dipping fries into ketchup.

Friend

Interlock index fingers and then reverse positions.

Frog

With fist under chin, quickly flick out first two fingers twice.

Fruit

Twist the "F" hand at side of chin.

Gentle

Using one hand, slowly stroke the back of the other.

Gift

Move both "X" hands from chest outward.

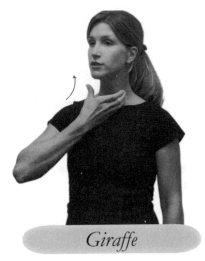

Giraffe

Move "C" hand from neck upward as if tracing the neck of a giraffe.

Girl

Trace jawline with thumb of "A" hand.

Go

Point both index fingers up and then point them outward.

Goat

Rest bent first two fingers at chin. While straightening fingers, move upward toward forehead.

Grandma

Place thumb of open hand on chin and arch outward two times.

Grandpa

Place thumb of open hand on forehead and arch outward two times.

Grapes

Bounce tips of curved fingers down the back of other hand from wrist to knuckles.

Green

Use "G" hand and shake slightly up and down.

Hair

Hold strand of hair between thumb and index finger.

Happy

Starting at chest, sweep
one or both flat hands in
small upward motions
several times.

Hat

Pat head to show where
a hat goes.

Help

Use one hand, open
palm, to lift fist of
other hand.

Home

Move closed fingertips
from side of mouth
upward to side of head.

Horse

Place thumb at forehead, moving first two fingers back and forth.

Hot

Cup hand at mouth, then move down and outward as if flinging hot food from mouth.

Hot dog

Squeeze both fists together, then open and close them as you move horizontally outward.

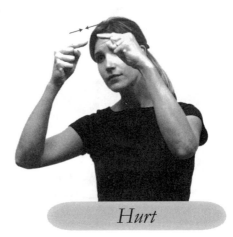

Hurt

Tap index fingers together near area of pain.

Ice cream

Hold imaginary cone
under chin and lick.

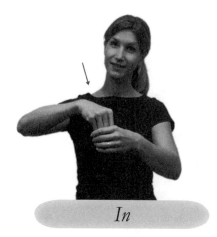

In

Put fingertips of one
hand into other "O"
hand.

Juice

Make "J" hand in front
of body.

Jump

Bend first two fingers
of one hand. "Jump"
up and down on palm of
other hand.

Key

Hold imaginary key and
twist in open palm of
other hand.

Light

Tap middle finger and
thumb to chin. Move
upward, opening and
extending fingers like
beams of light.

Lion

Starting at forehead with
fingers bent, pull hand
back and over head,
outlining lion's mane.

Little

Move hands toward
each other in small quick
movements.

Love

Cross fists over chest as
if hugging someone.

Medicine

Press and move slightly
the middle finger of
one hand into center of
other palm.

Milk

Open and close fist as if
milking a cow.

Mommy

Tap chin with thumb of
open hand.

Monkey

Scratch under arms with
one or both hands as a
monkey would.

Moon

Move "C" hand outward
from your eye to the sky.

More

Tap fingertips together.

Mouse

Brush end of nose with
index finger a few times.

Movie

Move open hand back and forth against other hand to mimic film moving through projector.

My/mine

Place open palm against chest.

Noise

Point index finger to ear, shake both "S" hands back and forth.

Orange

Squeeze fist in front of chin.

Outside

Close fingertips as hand
moves backward.

Pacifier

Place index finger and
thumb to mouth and
imitate sucking.

Pajamas

Fingerspell P-J and then
sign *clothes*.

Peas

Tap bent index finger
across "peapod" index
finger of other hand.

Pig

Place back of hand under chin and flap fingers up and down.

Pink

Brush middle finger of "P" hand down from lips several times.

Play

Shake both "Y" hands back and forth.

Please

With open hand, make circle around your heart.

Potty

Shake "T" hand (toilet)
back and forth.

Purple

Shake "P" hand back and
forth in front of body.

Rain

Wiggle fingertips and
move hands down
to mimic rainfall.

Red

Swipe index finger
downward from the
bottom lip.

Sad

With index finger, trace tears down face.

Shampoo

With bent hands, imitate washing hair.

Share

Slide right open hand (little finger down) along index finger of other open hand.

Sheep

With "K" hand, swipe up arm as if shearing a sheep.

Shoes

With knuckles up,
tap fists together
several times.

Sick

Place middle finger of
one hand on forehead
and middle finger of other
hand on stomach.

Sister

Touch chin with thumb of
right "L" hand and
move down to rest on
left "L" hand.

Sleep/bed

Form pillow with one or
both hands. Tilt and rest
head on hands.

Slide

Fingerspell S-L-I-D-E,
then move hand across
body as if sliding down a
slide.

Snow

Slowly wiggle fingers
downward and to the
side like falling, drifting
snow.

Soap

With fingertips of one
hand, stroke palm of
other hand.

Socks

Point index fingers down
and rub up and down
against each other.

Song

Wave open palm of one hand back and forth over inside of other extended arm.

Spaghetti

Start with two little fingers close together and move apart in circling motions.

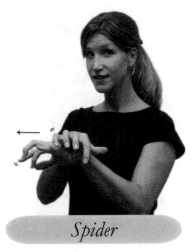

Spider

With one hand over the other, wiggle fingers as hands move sideways.

Squirrel

Tap two bent "V" hands together near mouth.

Stars

Point index fingers
toward the sky and move
them back and forth
against each other.

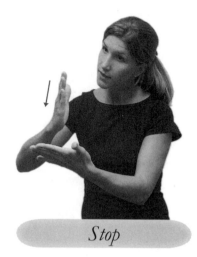

Stop

Sharply hit open palm
with side of other hand.

Sun

With index finger, draw
circle toward sky.
Then extend open
fingers toward head
like sun rays.

Swim

Imitate swimming the
breaststroke.

Swing

Place right first two
fingers on back of left
first two fingers. Swing
back and forth.

Telephone

Place thumb of "Y" hand
toward ear and little
finger toward mouth.

Thank you

Place fingertips on
chin and make arching
movement outward.

Toothbrush

Shake index finger up
and down in front of
open mouth.

Train

Place right first two
fingers on back of left
first two fingers. Slide
top fingers back
and forth.

Tree

Rest right elbow on back
of left hand. Spread right
fingers and rotate left
several times.

Turtle

Cover right fist with left
palm with right thumb
sticking out. Wiggle
thumb like turtle's head.

Vegetable

Make "V" hand at side of
mouth. Flip fingers back
and forth.

Walk

Point fingertips down
and alternately flap hands
back and forth.

Want

With palms up and
fingers curled, pull hands
in toward body.

Wash

With one fist up and
other down, rub together
in circular motion.

Watch/time

Tap back of wrist with
curved index finger.

Water

Tap index finger of "W" hand against side of mouth.

Where

Point index finger up and shake back and forth.

Yellow

Twist "Y" hand in front of body.

Yogurt

Using "Y" hand, scoop imaginary yogurt out of palm and up to mouth.

Zebra

With curved four fingers,
swipe across chest twice
to represent stripes.

Baby-Friendly Signs

Afraid

Pat chest rapidly.

Airplane

Raise arms straight out
to sides.

Ball

Throw pretend ball.

Bib

Tap chest with index finger.

Big

Reach arms up high.

Bird

Flap arms out at sides.

Bubbles

Pop imaginary rising
bubbles.

Bug

With thumb to finger,
move through air.

Bunny

Make V with fingers,
bounce several times.

Cereal

Use thumb and index
fingers to pick up
imaginary cereal.

Chicken

Place hands under shoulders and flap "wings."

Dance

Move torso and arms as if dancing.

Diaper

Pat hip.

Dog

Pant with tongue out.

Duck

Form bill with fingertips
and thumb, open and
close.

Elephant

Place fingertips on nose,
move arm up and down.

Fish

Smack lips several times.

Flower

Wrinkle nose and sniff
several times.

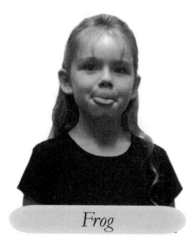

Frog

Move tongue in and out.

Good job!

Hold both thumbs up
and smile.

Horse

Hold "reins," bounce
torso up and down.

Hot

Blow out twice as if
cooling food.

Light

With hands at shoulder level, open and close fists.

Moon

Raise palm high and make circles.

Outside

Turn imaginary doorknob.

Pig

Press index finger to nose.

Spider

Twist tips of index
fingers together.

Stars

With hands up high,
wiggle fingers.

Stop

Push open palm forward.

Sun

Curve both arms over
head.

Swing

Hold "ropes" and
rock torso.

Telephone

Place fist to ear.

Train

Move fist up and down
pulling whistle.

Wash

Rub palms against
each other.

Where

Hold upturned palms out
to sides.

Alphabet

A

B

C

D

E

F

G

H

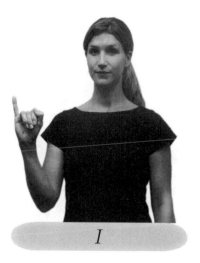

I

J

K

L

M

N

O

P

Q

R

S

T

U

V

W

X

Y

Z

Baby Signs Resources

IN RESPONSE TO REQUESTS FROM PARENTS FOR MATERIALS TO make learning signs fun and easy, we have created a wide variety of high-quality developmentally appropriate classes and products. Brief summaries of these resources are provided in this appendix; details are available on our website, www.babysigns.com.

Baby Signs Workshops and Classes

Our workshops and classes are taught by a nationwide network of Baby Signs independent certified instructors. They include:

- The Baby Signs Parent Workshop, designed to introduce families to the Baby Signs program
- Two sets of classes for babies and parents to attend together called Sign, Say & Play and More Sign, Say & Play
- The Baby Signs Early Childhood Educator (ECE) Training, designed to help early childhood education professionals incorporate the program into large and small childcare settings
- Baby Signs potty training program classes (Potty Training Made Easy with the Baby Signs Program), designed to introduce families to this innovative and effective program that brings the magic of signing to a challenge that all parents face

Baby Signs Signing Products

A wide variety of signing resources for children, parents, and early childhood educators are available on our website and through our instructors. These products include:

- Books and video dictionaries for parents
- Books and DVDs for babies
- Theme-based Fun Packs for babies
  (DVD, book, and chubby flash cards)
- Sign, Say & Play kits (DVD, book, music CD, and more)
- BeeBo the Baby Signs Bear
- Baby Signs potty training kit
- Quick reference guides
- Classroom kits for large and small childcare settings

Also Available at www.babysigns.com

- **Baby Signs Career Opportunity.** Join our Baby Signs Independent Certified Instructor Program and help us spread the good news about signing through your own home-based business.

- **The Baby Signs Parent Newsletter.** Keep up-to-date on signs for holidays, new products, and fun signing activities by subscribing to our newsletter.

- *Baby Minds: Brain-Building Games Your Baby Will Love.* Learn about our second research-based parenting book (Bantam, 2000), in which we share fascinating facts about intellectual development during the first three years of life. The book also includes dozens of tips on how parents and educators can use this information to make playtime fun as well as educational.

- *Baby Hearts: A Guide to Giving Your Child an Emotional Head Start.* Learn about our third research-based book for parents (Bantam, 2005), in which we describe extraordinary new research findings about the emotional awareness of children during the earliest years of life and the importance of cultivating these inborn abilities. Once again, we translate the research into terms parents can appreciate and provide lots of strategies and games that parents can use to foster their child's emotional well-being.

About the Authors

LINDA ACREDOLO, PH.D., professor emeritus of psychology at the University of California, Davis, is an internationally recognized scholar in the field of child development. A Phi Beta Kappa graduate of Bucknell University, she earned her Ph.D. in child development from the University of Minnesota. Dr. Acredolo is a fellow of both the American Psychological Association and the American Psychological Society, has served as associate editor of the prestigious journal *Child Development*, and is a member of the *Parents* magazine advisory board. Dr. Acredolo lives with her husband in Woodland, California.

SUSAN GOODWYN, PH.D., professor emeritus of psychology at the California State University at Stanislaus, received her masters of science with first honors from the University of London and her Ph.D. in psychology from the University of California, Davis. Dr. Goodwyn has an outstanding research record, having served as project director and co-principal investigator for two major grants, one sponsored by the National Institutes of Health and the other by the Kellogg Foundation. Dr. Goodwyn lives with her husband in Vacaville, California.

DRS. ACREDOLO AND GOODWYN are cofounders of Baby Signs, Inc., and its educational arm, the Baby Signs Institute. The institute represents the product of their two decades of research devoted to determining the effect on infants and toddlers of using signs to communicate before they can talk. Major funding for this work was received from the National Institutes of Health. The results of their research attesting to the positive effects of signing on development have appeared in peer-reviewed professional journals and books and have been presented at over thirty national and international conferences. Determined to spread the good news beyond academia, in 1996 Drs. Acredolo and Goodwyn coauthored the first edition of this landmark book for parents. Since that time they have worked tirelessly to share the Baby Signs program with as many families as possible around the world.

DOUGLAS ABRAMS is a writer and editor and founding partner of Idea Architects, a creative book and media development company. His twin daughters, Kayla and Eliana, were enthusiastic devotees of the Baby Signs program. He worked with Drs. Acredolo and Goodwyn to prepare this new edition and to develop the signing board book series published by Harper-Collins.

A Trilogy of Research-Based Advice for Parents

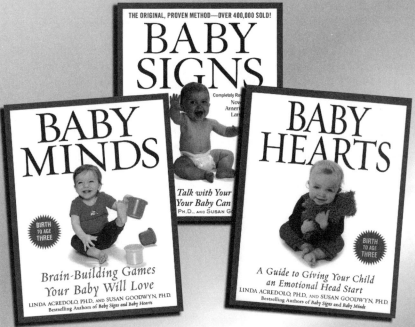

by

Linda Acredolo, Ph.D., & Susan Goodwyn, Ph.D.

sign language for babies

For information on educational programs, related products, and career opportunities, contact Baby Signs, Inc., at (800) 995-0226 or visit www.babysigns.com.